PRESENTED TO

_____

BY

_____

DATE

_____

180
DEVOTIONS
ON
COURAGE
→ FOR
MEN

180 DEVOTIONS ON COURAGE FOR MEN

FEATURING CONTEMPORARY READINGS AND CLASSICS FROM MOODY, SPURGEON, WESLEY, AND MURRAY

BARBOUR
PUBLISHING

Scripture quotations marked KJV are taken from the King James Version of the Bible.

Scripture quotations marked SKJV are taken from the Barbour Simplified KJV, copyright © 2022 by Barbour Publishing, Inc., Uhrichsville, Ohio 44683. All rights reserved.

Scripture quotations marked NIV are taken from the Holy Bible, NEW INTERNATIONAL VERSION®. NIV®. Copyright © 1973, 1978, 1984, 2011 by Biblica, Inc.™ Used by permission. All rights reserved worldwide.

Scripture quotations marked NLT are taken from the *Holy Bible*. New Living Translation copyright © 1996, 2004, 2015 by Tyndale House Foundation. Used by permission of Tyndale House Publishers, Inc. Carol Stream, Illinois 60188. All rights reserved.

Scripture quotations marked MSG are from *THE MESSAGE*. Copyright © by Eugene H. Peterson 1993, 1994, 1995, 1996, 2000, 2001, 2002. Used by permission of NavPress Publishing Group.

Cover Design: Greg Jackson, Thinkpen Design

Published by Barbour Publishing, Inc., 1810 Barbour Drive, Uhrichsville, Ohio 44683, www.barbourbooks.com

Our mission is to inspire the world with the life-changing message of the Bible.

Member of the
Evangelical Christian
Publishers Association

Printed in China.

LIFE GETS REALLY HARD SOMETIMES. BUT CHRISTIAN MEN CAN FACE EVERY CHALLENGE WITH COURAGE.

This 180-entry devotional builds off the inspired message of 2 Corinthians 12:10 (NIV):

For Christ's sake, I delight in weaknesses,
in insults, in hardships, in persecutions, in difficulties.
For when I am weak, then I am strong.

Featuring both contemporary entries and "classics" from figures such as D. L. Moody, Andrew Murray, Charles Spurgeon, and John Wesley, *180 Devotions on Courage for Men* promises insight and inspiration for guys of all ages.

Whatever life is throwing at you, you'll be encouraged to seek your daily strength from God the Father through His Son, Jesus Christ. Sure, life can be tough. But with the all-powerful God on your side, how can you be anything but courageous?

JOSEPH'S CHOICE

Joseph, to whom she was engaged, was a righteous man and did not want to disgrace her publicly, so he decided to break the engagement quietly. As he considered this, an angel of the Lord appeared to him in a dream. "Joseph, son of David," the angel said, "do not be afraid to take Mary as your wife. For the child within her was conceived by the Holy Spirit."

MATTHEW 1:19–20 NLT

Joseph, a working-class man, didn't expect drama when he invited Mary to be his wife. Then Mary got pregnant and Joseph found himself in a frightening situation.

If Mary was unfaithful in their engagement, might she be unfaithful during their marriage? Would the community assume Joseph had had premarital sexual relations? What if the baby looked nothing like Joseph? Mary's infidelity might become obvious, and people would shun the couple. Joseph's livelihood in carpentry might be jeopardized.

So he decided to break things off. If Joseph did that publicly, Mary's infidelity would be punishable by death. If he divorced her quietly, she would be shamed, but live. Joseph held Mary's life—and the life of her unborn child—in his hands.

Then an angel appeared. Joseph was to marry Mary as planned. He was to trust God over the evidence of Mary's seeming infidelity.

Perhaps the angel's request—God's request—seemed unfair to Joseph. There will be times when God's expectations of us will be tough too. Will we choose to trust anyway? Joseph did. So can we.

THE LORD HIMSELF IS MY SALVATION

"Surely God is my salvation; I will trust and not be afraid. The LORD, the LORD himself, is my strength and my defense; he has become my salvation."

ISAIAH 12:2 NIV

Isaiah 12 is essentially tied with Jeremiah 45 as the shortest chapter in all the books of the prophets. But "small" doesn't imply "weak." The theme of Isaiah 12—praising the Lord for being Israel's salvation—foreshadows the great prophecies of the Messiah in Isaiah 40 and following.

Today's verse spells out some practical implications of praising the Lord, and each is more relevant today than ever.

First, trust in the Lord. Know that He is bigger and stronger than any current national or international upheaval, personal uncertainty, or other dire circumstance.

Second, don't be afraid. In Isaiah's day, the Babylonians, Persians, or Medes were the issue; in our day, it may be foreign nations, climate change, disease, you name it. Isaiah says we can choose not to fear.

Third, grab hold of God's strength. This reminds us of Paul's affirmation, "I can do all things through Christ who strengthens me" (Philippians 4:13 SKJV). That is, the apostle could do each thing he had just commanded the believers of Philippi to do.

Fourth, appreciate God's protection. Know that death cannot touch us until the Lord's appointed time—until then, He defends us every second.

These truths will give us the strength to face the worst life throws at us.

FAITH IN MOTION

After saying this, he was taken up into a cloud while they were watching, and they could no longer see him. As they strained to see him rising into heaven, two white-robed men suddenly stood among them. "Men of Galilee," they said, "why are you standing here staring into heaven? Jesus has been taken from you into heaven, but someday he will return from heaven in the same way you saw him go!"

ACTS 1:9–11 NLT

After Jesus' work on earth was over, He ascended into heaven. The disciples watched Him leave, staring up into the sky even after He was completely out of sight. Were they hoping for another glimpse? The disciples stood and looked for so long that God sent two angels to tell them to move. Their apprenticeship was over. It was time to do the work their Lord had called them to do.

When God asks *us* to work, we may be tempted to stand still and continue to look for absolute clarity. How often do we hope that God will give us more instruction or make our pathway absolutely certain? But the apostle Paul has written, "We live by faith, not by sight" (2 Corinthians 5:7 NIV). In other words, as followers of Christ we move through life one faithful step at a time.

To keep us from staring up into the clouds—to get us moving in our work—Jesus uses words like *ask, seek,* and *knock* (Matthew 7:7). These active words build motion into our faith. And we live *by* faith, trusting and following our Lord even when we might wish for more sight.

THE REWARD WILL COME

And let us not be weary in doing good,
for in due season we shall reap, if we do not faint.
GALATIANS 6:9 SKJV

Don't let anybody fool you: the Christian life is tough. If it weren't, why would the apostle Paul write what he did in Galatians 6:9?

There is a weariness in well doing. There are those moments when we feel like fainting—or giving up, as other translations of the Bible say. In the context, Paul was describing the difficulties of restoring a fellow Christian who's fallen into sin. We are to carry each other's burden to fulfill the law of Christ (verse 2). But we must beware of the danger of falling into sin ourselves, perhaps by thinking we are better than our sinning brother (verses 1, 4).

This is the well-known passage that describes sowing and reaping, spiritually speaking: "Do not be deceived; God is not mocked, for whatever a man sows, that he shall also reap" (verse 7 SKJV). It's all work! Sowing, reaping, restoring fellow believers who stumble. . .

The good news is in verse 9, where Paul—speaking for God—promises a harvest. There will be a payoff for the hard work we put into our Christian lives. But we can't faint. We don't dare give up. Stay on task, do your work faithfully, allow God to strengthen you. . .and then wait for the reward. It will come.

THE LONG VICTORY

*Joshua waged war against all these kings for a
long time. . . . For it was the LORD himself who
hardened their hearts to wage war against Israel.*

JOSHUA 11:18, 20 NIV

Various sources suggest it took Joshua and his men five
to seven years to conquer the kings of northern Canaan.
That was a long time, but it makes sense, given that the
Israelites started in the south. By the time they reached the
north, the enemy kings—having heard of the Israelites'
advance—had probably dug in and formed alliances.

Notice that the Lord Himself hardened the kings'
hearts, causing them to wage war against Israel. But these
nations in the north were destined to fall. In Deuteronomy
31:8, Moses made a comforting promise to Joshua: "The
LORD himself goes before you and will be with you; he
will never leave you nor forsake you. Do not be afraid;
do not be discouraged" (NIV). Still, it took Joshua and his
army *years* to conquer their enemies. Not even a promised
victory was instantaneous. That's often the case for us too.

Have you been fighting a spiritual battle for years,
only to become discouraged by your lack of victory? As
soldiers in the fight, our job is to obey our commander
and leave the result to Him—no matter how long it takes.

Today, take heart. God goes before you and He will
be with you.

OFTEN AND LONG ALONE WITH GOD

"Speak to all the congregation of the children of Israel and say to them: 'You shall be holy, for I the LORD your God am holy.'"

LEVITICUS 19:2 SKJV

If you wish to strengthen yourself in the practice of this holy Presence, take up the holy Word. Take, for instance, the book of Leviticus and notice how God seven times gives the command: "Ye shall be holy, for I am holy.". . . Nothing but the knowledge of God, as the Holy One, will make us holy.

And how are we to obtain that knowledge of God, save in the Inner Chamber? It is a thing utterly impossible unless we take time and allow the holiness of God to shine on us. How can any man on earth obtain intimate knowledge of another man of remarkable wisdom if he does not associate with him and place himself under his influence? And how can God Himself sanctify us if we do not take time to be brought under the power of the glory of His holiness?

Nowhere can we get to know the holiness of God and come under its influence and power save in the Inner Chamber. It has been well said: "No man can expect to make progress in holiness who is not often and long alone with God."

WILL WE SAY YES?

This is what the Sovereign LORD, the Holy One of Israel,
says: "In repentance and rest is your salvation, in quietness
and trust is your strength, but you would have none of it."

ISAIAH 30:15 NIV

In Isaiah 30 and 31, the Lord drives home a point to His people Israel: it's futile and absurd to rely on Egypt for salvation from the upcoming Babylonian conquest. What in the world could Pharaoh and his armies do to save the Israelites? Human power is nothing compared to the infinite and eternal greatness of the Lord God.

Two descriptions of God echo throughout this section of Isaiah. The first is "the Sovereign LORD" or "LORD Almighty"; the second is "the Holy One of Israel." How good that we can know God in His sovereignty (greatness), providence (goodness and guidance), holiness (glory), love (graciousness), and mystery ("God alone knows").

Do these descriptions of the Lord God move our souls and echo from our lips? If yes, we will have the strength to face any and every challenge that comes our way. If no, what futile and absurd plan are we pursuing?

Scripture, history, and contemporary experience all call us to rely on the Lord alone. How do we do that? Today's verse prescribes repentance (confession of sin), rest (in God Himself), quietness (while waiting for His salvation), and trust (focusing on the Lord and no one else). How heartbreaking to see the prophet's words, "but you would have none of it." May that never be true of us!

SHADOWS AND LIGHT

Yes, though I walk through the valley of the shadow
of death, I will not fear evil, for You are with me.
Your rod and Your staff, they comfort me. You prepare
a table before me in the presence of my enemies. You
anoint my head with oil. My cup runs over. Surely
goodness and mercy shall follow me all the days of my
life, and I will dwell in the house of the LORD *forever.*

PSALM 23:4–6 SKJV

Fear is like a shadow. It's a small thing. But when we give it permission to stand in front of the light of Christ, it will block that light and spread a terrifying blackness over our lives. This shadow deceiver can cause a legitimate panic that rages like wildfire, jumping from one light-starved heart to another. When we focus on the growing darkness the shadow creates, we can find ourselves paralyzed by an enemy that looks unassailable—but does not even exist.

When our peace fades into the shadows, the solution lies in removing the darkness that stands in front of God's Word. The only way that Satan's lies can block the light is if we allow them to—if we seek the lies, rather than God's kingdom—first.

When you are God's child, you can claim His presence and protection in any and every situation. . .up to and including the valley of the shadow of death.

GOD IS MORE WILLING TO BLESS

And when I came to you, brothers, I did not come with excellency of speech or of wisdom declaring to you the testimony of God. For I determined not to know anything among you except Jesus Christ and Him crucified.

1 CORINTHIANS 2:1–2 SKJV

It was not enticing words; it was not eloquence that Paul had. Why, he said his speech was contemptible! He did not profess to be an orator; but he preached Christ, the power of God and the wisdom of God, Christ and Him crucified.

And this is what the whole world wants—Christ and Him crucified. And the world will perish for want of Christ. Let every man and woman that loves the Lord Jesus begin to publish the tidings of salvation. Talk to your neighbors and your friends. Run and speak to that young man! Talk to him of heaven and of the love of Christ! Tell him that you want to see him saved; and bear in mind this, that God is far more willing to bless us than we are to have Him.

Let us then keep close to Christ.

THE SAME SPIRIT

As soon as Jesus was baptized, he went up out of the
water. At that moment heaven was opened, and he saw
the Spirit of God descending like a dove and alighting
on him. And a voice from heaven said, "This is my
Son, whom I love; with him I am well pleased."
MATTHEW 3:16–17 NIV

Jesus' baptism, mentioned in all four Gospels, precedes
His formal ministry. It is one of the few situations in scripture depicting the Trinity together. As Jesus came out of
the water, the Holy Spirit descended from heaven and the
Father audibly declared His love.

The spoken declaration calls to mind Isaiah 42:1,
which says, "Here is my servant, whom I uphold, my
chosen one in whom I delight; I will put my Spirit on him,
and he will bring justice to the nations" (NIV).

Observers on the shore watched as Jesus stepped into
His role as justice bringer, endorsed by God the Father and
empowered by the Holy Spirit. People may have assumed
Jesus' baptism would be followed by a dramatic march to
Rome, where He would overthrow the emperor and take
His rightful place as ruler. Instead, Jesus went into the
wilderness to be tempted by the devil.

Though His ministry defied human expectations, Jesus
did bring justice to the nations: He satisfied His Father's
justice by being a worthy sacrifice for human sin. Jesus'
strength was shown in the form of weakness.

Now, if we are willing to show weakness and admit
we need a savior, the same Holy Spirit that descended on
Jesus will empower us.

LOOK BEYOND THE STARS TO GOD

*Who has measured the waters in the hollow of His
hand, and measured out heaven with a span?*

ISAIAH 40:12 SKJV

God's greatness can be compared to the vastness of space.
Today, our basic unit of measurement is a foot. In ancient
times, it was a span, the width of a hand from the end
of the thumb to the tip of the little finger—a distance of
about nine inches.

If we were to mark off the distance from here to the
moon by spans, it would take more than fifty years to do
it. . .assuming someone could mark a span every second
of every minute of every hour of every day of every week
of every month for every one of those years. Yet in no time,
the Lord God marked off every span across the universe,
nearly 100 billion light-years (as far as we can tell right
now). Beyond that, He knows each of the countless billions
of stars by name (Isaiah 40:26).

The point isn't just that the Lord is a lot smarter
than us. He is infinitely and completely beyond us. God
didn't go to school to learn how to make a universe. He
didn't have to read a book to know how to keep the entire
cosmos running. He never had to learn, because He is
the all-knowing, all-powerful sovereign of all.

No one will ever explain to God a better way to run
human lives, no matter how hard they try. So relax and let
Him lead. If He can manage the universe, He can handle
your circumstances.

GOD HAS THE POWER

While the man held on to Peter and John, all the
people were astonished and came running to them in
the place called Solomon's Colonnade. When Peter saw
this, he said to them: "Fellow Israelites, why does this
surprise you? Why do you stare at us as if by our own
power or godliness we had made this man walk?"

ACTS 3:11–12 NIV

Peter and John were two of Jesus' closest disciples. They were taught by the greatest teacher in the world, God in flesh. They were given the Holy Spirit to equip them to carry out God's plans. It could have been easy for Peter and John to become arrogant. Instead, they gave glory to God, knowing full well the power behind their miracles was the heavenly Father.

Unfortunately, we don't always see miracles in our daily experience.

When we experience a life-altering event like a job loss or a troubling diagnosis, it's easy to succumb to a sense of hopelessness. We may think we'll never get out of our pit of hardship. We feel powerless to do anything but sulk.

But just as God was with Peter and John, He is with us too. We don't have to pull ourselves out of our circumstances. As believers in Jesus, we can call on His name and power to do the heavy lifting. The God who had power to let the blind see, the lame walk, and the dead rise to life two thousand years ago still has that power today. And He will give us strength to weather whatever storms our life can muster.

RUN TO CHRIST

*The LORD said to Joshua, "Now tell the Israelites to
designate the cities of refuge, as I instructed Moses.
Anyone who kills another person accidentally and
unintentionally can run to one of these cities."*

JOSHUA 20:1–3 NLT

At God's instruction, Israel chose six sanctuary cities
that were spread out across Canaan. If an Israelite took
someone's life by accident, he or she could flee to one of
these cities for protection from an avenger. (You can learn
more about the sanctuary cities in Numbers 35:9–15.)

These special cities protected anyone who had killed
another person unintentionally. But the killer could be
avenged legally if he chose to go outside the city. The
sanctuary was always available, but never to be disregarded.

Today, Christians know how often they sin—both
unintentionally and with full knowledge. Some days are
better than others, and some more challenging. We all
fight against the "old man" and the wickedness of our own
hearts every day. As the prophet Jeremiah said, "The human
heart is the most deceitful of all things, and desperately
wicked. Who really knows how bad it is?" (17:9 NLT).

That's the bad news. The good news is this: even
when we've failed for the hundredth (or thousandth)
time, we can always run to Jesus to confess our sins. He
is our sanctuary city.

THE CREATOR
IS YOUR GUIDE

*"And they will tell it to the inhabitants of this land.
For they have heard that You, LORD, are among
these people, that You, LORD, are seen face to
face and that Your cloud stands over them, and
that You go before them in a pillar of a cloud by
day time and in a pillar of fire by night."*

NUMBERS 14:14 SKJV

All that the children of Israel had to do in the wilderness
was to follow the cloud. If the cloud rested, they rested;
if the cloud moved forward, then they moved as it did. I
can imagine the first thing Moses, or any of the people,
did, when the gray dawn of morning broke, was to look
up and see if the cloud was still over the camp. By night
it was a pillar of fire, lighting up the camp and filling
them with a sense of God's protecting care; by day it was
a cloud, shielding them from the fierce heat of the sun's
rays and sheltering them from the sight of their enemies.

Israel's Shepherd could lead His people through the
pathless desert. Why? Because He made it. He knew every
grain of sand in it. They could not have had a better leader
through the wilderness than its Creator.

STRENGTH IN SURRENDER

Finally, my brothers, be strong in the
Lord and in the power of His might.
EPHESIANS 6:10 SKJV

Men, generally speaking, like to be in control. From earliest childhood, we like to say, "I can do it myself!" All through life, we want to impress others with our own strength—physical, emotional, intellectual, even spiritual. But God's ways are often very different from ours (see Isaiah 55:8). He calls us to surrender.

God does assign certain tasks to us, giving us areas of responsibility. We are expected to do our best, develop our gifts, and accomplish as much as we can for His glory. But we are never in total control. Our strength comes from God, from the power of *His* might. Many centuries before the apostle Paul wrote to the Ephesians, Moses was telling the ancient Israelites, "But you shall remember the LORD your God, for it is He who gives you power to get wealth" (Deuteronomy 8:18 SKJV).

Christians walk a fine line. We are supposed to work. We are called to be strong. But the strength for our work always comes from God, and He gives that strength as we surrender to Him. Surrendering is choosing to obey or follow someone or something other than yourself. As Paul wrote elsewhere, "Don't you realize that you become the slave of whatever you choose to obey? You can be a slave to sin, which leads to death, or you can choose to obey God, which leads to righteous living" (Romans 6:16 NLT). Our strength comes from choosing to follow Christ.

WILDERNESS EXPERIENCES

*Then Jesus was led by the Spirit into the wilderness
to be tempted there by the devil. For forty days and
forty nights he fasted and became very hungry.*
MATTHEW 4:1–2 NLT

Immediately following His baptism, Jesus was led to the
wilderness. It seems like a strange way to begin His earthly
ministry: the heavens had just opened and declared Jesus
to be God's Son in whom He was well pleased. Jesus could
have immediately started healing the sick and cleaning
out the temple, but the Holy Spirit led Him into the
wastelands, where He would encounter hardship, hunger,
and temptation.

Life is sometimes like that. We can experience a
spiritual high on Sunday, when it feels like the heavens
opened and God declared His love for us. Then Monday,
back in the regular routine, we feel hungry, spiritually
bereft, and tempted by the devil to lay aside our mission.

If Jesus experienced such wilderness moments,
shouldn't we as His followers expect to encounter them
as well? And since Jesus overcame His trials, we can claim
His victory too. We can respond to temptation with God's
truth. Our spiritual hunger is satisfied by His Word. Our
hardships end when we follow Him home.

In this life, there's always a wilderness. But it plays a
valuable role in our growth. Once we learn that the source
of our strength is not in ourselves but in the power of
God's Word, we will be ready for the ministry God has
prepared for us.

GOD IS WORTHY
OF OUR TRUST

"Though He slay me, I will still trust in Him."
JOB 13:15 SKJV

What a sweet word is that word *trust*! But there are some things we must not trust. The reason many are in darkness is because they trust in doctrines, in creeds or ordinances, instead of in their Lord and Savior Jesus Christ.

A man said to me lately he could not trust himself. We are not required to do that, for our hearts are deceitful above all things and desperately wicked. But there is no reason why we should not trust God. God is worthy of our trust; He is always faithful. Our nearest friends may deceive us, but God never will.

God will keep them in perfect peace whose minds are stayed on Him (Isaiah 26:3). We must be able to say with Job, "Though He slay me, yet will I trust in Him." If God cannot be trusted, whom can we trust? Unbelief is more than a misfortune; it is a dreadful sin. We must learn to trust, even where we cannot see, and with all our heart. . .not a half-hearted trust. The fruits of trusting are peace, joy, happiness, and mercy. Who would not trust God?

GOD'S HAND LOCKS ONTO OURS

"So do not fear, for I am with you; do not be dismayed,
for I am your God. I will strengthen you and help you;
I will uphold you with my righteous right hand. . . .
For I am the LORD your God who takes hold of your
right hand and says to you, Do not fear; I will help you."

ISAIAH 41:10, 13 NIV

The Lord wants to take hold of your right hand in challenging, difficult, and dangerous circumstances. While God said that Job's own right hand couldn't save him (Job 40:9–14), the Lord's certainly could. From Psalm 60 to 139, we repeatedly hear that God's right hand reaches down to save those He loves and redeems. We hear a similar promise in Isaiah 41–42.

Perhaps the most thrilling picture of God's hand at work is found in Matthew 14:28–31. That's when Jesus, miraculously walking on the Sea of Galilee, is joined briefly by the impetuous Peter. When he lets his focus drift from Jesus to the storm, Peter immediately sinks. But Jesus reaches out His hand, grabs Peter's, and pulls him up and out of the water. How strong Jesus is! And how electrifying it must have felt when Jesus locked onto Peter's outstretched hand.

Why would Jesus save the impulsive apostle? To bless Peter. To rededicate him for the Lord's service. To draw Peter even closer to his Savior. To redeem Peter physically only a few dozen verses before his amazing confession of faith: "You [Jesus] are the Messiah, the Son of the living God" (Matthew 16:16 NIV).

Jesus is ready and willing to save us too. Just reach out your hand!

PROVIDER IN ADVERSITY

The priests and the captain of the temple guard and the Sadducees came up to Peter and John while they were speaking to the people. They were greatly disturbed because the apostles were teaching the people, proclaiming in Jesus the resurrection of the dead. They seized Peter and John and, because it was evening, they put them in jail until the next day. But many who heard the message believed; so the number of men who believed grew to about five thousand.

Acts 4:1–4 niv

Before Jesus ascended to the Father, He gave His followers the Great Commission: "Therefore go and make disciples of all nations, baptizing them in the name of the Father and of the Son and of the Holy Spirit" (Matthew 28:19 niv). Peter and John did precisely what our Lord commanded them to do. The result was immediate opposition.

Have you ever experienced that? You felt you were precisely where God called you to be, but you faced consistent obstacles? This might be the exact result of closely following Jesus. After all, the Lord did tell His followers, "In this world you will have trouble" (John 16:33 niv). When we share the gospel or choose to stand with Christ, adversity is not a possibility but an inevitability.

The good news is that the God we serve gave manna to the Israelites in the desert (Exodus 16). He provided other miraculous bread to an exhausted Elijah (1 Kings 17:2–6). And He will give us everything we need to accomplish our calling. As Jesus reminds us in Matthew 28:20 (niv), "surely I am with you always, to the very end of the age."

TOUCH, TAKE HOLD, TAKE FAST HOLD

Take fast hold of instruction; do not let
her go. Keep her, for she is your life.
PROVERBS 4:13 SKJV

Faith may be well described as taking hold upon divine instruction. God has condescended to teach us, and it is ours to hear with attention and receive His words; and while we are hearing faith comes, even that faith which saves the soul.

To take "fast hold" is an exhortation which concerns the strength, the reality, the heartiness, and the truthfulness of faith, and the more of these the better. If to take hold is good, to take fast hold is better. Even a touch of the hem of Christ's garment causeth healing to come to us, but if we want the full riches which are treasured up in Christ, we must not only touch but take hold; and if we would know from day to day to the very uttermost all the fullness of His grace, we must take fast hold, and so maintain a constant and close connection between our souls and the eternal fountain of life.

It were well to give such a grip as a man gives to a plank when he seizes hold upon it for his very life—that is a fast hold indeed.

LIVING FOR CHRIST

For to me to live is Christ,
and to die is gain.

PHILIPPIANS 1:21 SKJV

As he wrote his letter to the Philippians, the apostle Paul was in prison for preaching the gospel. His survival strategy was two-pronged: sharing Jesus no matter what and anticipating the moment he would enter into glory. As long as Paul had air to breathe, nothing could stop him from preaching Christ. After that, he'd be *with* Christ.

Even in confinement he pressed on, writing letters to individual believers and to churches—"epistles" that still speak to Christians today as books of the New Testament. Paul's unwavering commitment to Jesus, even in a prison cell, stimulated other believers to share the gospel more boldly (verse 14). In some of the most difficult situations imaginable, Paul never stopped living for Christ, knowing that one day he would see Jesus face to face.

That perspective can overcome all the disappointments, hardships, and pain of this life. No matter how daunting or lengthy our challenges may be—and some are incredibly heavy—a focus on Jesus will provide the strength we need to get through.

As long as there's breath in your lungs, live for Christ. Death just means you'll be alive in His presence.

JUST GO

So Abram went, as the LORD had told him.
GENESIS 12:4 NIV

In terms of its wording, today's verse is simple enough for a beginning reader. But many of us would find the calling of Abram an incredible challenge.

As a seventy-five-year-old man, Abram got a visit from God along with a command: "Go from your country, your people and your father's household to the land I will show you" (Genesis 12:1 NIV). And, just like that, Abram obeyed.

God's call and Abram's response bookend a remarkable promise the Lord made. "I will make you into a great nation, and I will bless you," God said. "I will make your name great, and you will be a blessing. I will bless those who bless you, and whoever curses you I will curse; and all peoples on earth will be blessed through you" (Genesis 12:2–3 NIV).

As He did with Abram, the Lord calls us to various tasks—in our homes, our churches, and our communities. And He makes us remarkable promises as well, including this one: "Never will I leave you; never will I forsake you" (Hebrews 13:5 NIV).

The key for us is to obey. When God's will is clear, whether through a teaching of scripture or a specific call on our lives (which will always align with the teaching of scripture), we must be like Abraham and just go. God will take care of the rest.

CRY OUT FOR MERCY

Whenever the L<small>ORD</small> raised up a judge over Israel,
he was with that judge and rescued the people
from their enemies throughout the judge's lifetime.
For the L<small>ORD</small> took pity on his people, who were
burdened by oppression and suffering.

<small>JUDGES 2:18 NLT</small>

Judges 2 contains one of the saddest verses in the Bible. Following the death of Joshua and all his contemporaries, "after that generation died, another generation grew up who did not acknowledge the L<small>ORD</small> or remember the mighty things he had done for Israel" (verse 10 <small>NLT</small>). Apparently, the stories of God's faithfulness had not been passed down, so the people did what came naturally. They served other gods and they faced God's punishment.

But in their ignorance and weakness and trouble, God showed the Israelites pity by saving them from their enemies. Judgment is in God's nature, but so is mercy—especially when He sees His chosen ones suffering, even when it's of their own doing.

Perhaps you're going through a dry period in your spiritual walk. When you avoid God, you become easy pickings for Satan. But if you cry out to God for mercy, He'll grant it quickly.

If, like the prodigal son, you ever find yourself in a pigpen of your own making, don't hesitate to call out to the Father. He will lift you up, clean you off, and embrace you in love.

MINDS STAYED ON JESUS

But let all those who put their trust in You rejoice.
Let them ever shout for joy because You defend them.
Let those also who love Your name be joyful in You.

PSALM 5:11 SKJV

When it is dark and stormy here, strive to rise higher and higher, near to Christ, and you will find it all calm there. You know that it is the highest mountain peaks that catch the first rays of the sun. So those who rise highest catch the first news from heaven.

It is those sunny Christians who go through the world with smiles on their faces that win souls. And, on the other hand, it is those Christians who go through the world hanging their heads like bulrushes that scare people away from religion. Why, it's a libel on Christianity for a religious man to go about with such a downcast look.

What does the Master say? "My joy I leave with you, my joy I give unto you" (see John 15:11). Depend upon it, if our minds were stayed upon Him, we should have perfect peace, and with perfect peace we should have perfect joy.

SURRENDER THE SITUATION

"Therefore, in the present case I advise you: Leave these men alone! Let them go! For if their purpose or activity is of human origin, it will fail. But if it is from God, you will not be able to stop these men; you will only find yourselves fighting against God."

ACTS 5:38–39 NIV

Gamaliel had seen this before: Theudas and then Judas the Galilean claimed to be men of significance. They were killed and their followers scattered.

But with Jesus' apostles it was different. Long after Jesus' death on a cross, His followers were bolder than ever. This prompted Gamaliel, a Pharisee and "a teacher of the law, who was honored by all the people" (Acts 5:34 NIV), to advise the Sanhedrin to leave Peter and the apostles alone. If God was with these men, they would prevail no matter what the Sanhedrin wanted to do about them.

Gamaliel is mentioned only briefly in scripture, but his message is profound, even in our day. Instead of taking matters into our own hands, using whatever social, political, or spiritual clout we think we have, trust that God knows best.

This is an act of surrender and deep trust in our heavenly Father. Whatever we might think we can do to get out of a difficult situation, it's best to simply give it over to God to do with as He wills. As the apostle Paul said, "when I am weak, then I am strong" (2 Corinthians 12:10 NIV).

YOU DON'T HAVE TO BE A STAR

Then Peter said to them, "Repent, and every one of you be baptized in the name of Jesus Christ. . . . Then those who gladly received his word were baptized, and the same day about three thousand souls were added to them.

ACTS 2:38, 41 SKJV

Though Jesus taught that His followers should be "servant of all" (Mark 9:35, 10:44 SKJV), our culture encourages and celebrates stardom. To be considered a success, you must be at the top of the mountain.

Sometimes, this attitude even colors our Christian lives. If we don't lead an organization, speak in front of crowds, or find ourselves in some other notable public position, we might feel like we're failing God. Or, perhaps, failing ourselves.

But the birth of the Christian church in Acts 2 provides a good counterbalance to these fears. Notice that Peter—who was certainly in a notable position—preached a message that led to the salvation of three thousand people. Though it's possible that some of their names appear throughout the New Testament letters written in following decades, we really know almost nothing about these early believers. Their average, everyday Christian lives, though, lived out in a very hostile culture, caused others to accept the gospel message, and that pattern repeated itself down to the current day. Your own salvation is likely part of a long chain of testimony dating to this moment in Acts 2.

You don't have to be a star to be a good Christian. God gave us the story of these early believers to encourage simple, everyday obedience.

GOD IS OUR MAKER

No one is like you, LORD; you are great, and your name is mighty in power. . . . God made the earth by his power; he founded the world by his wisdom and stretched out the heavens by his understanding. . . . "With my great power and outstretched arm I made the earth and its people and the animals that are on it, and I give it to anyone I please."

JEREMIAH 10:6, 12; 27:5 NIV

When God's Word stutters, we need to listen! Jeremiah repeatedly writes of the Lord's great power and wisdom in making the heavens and earth. Only God could have created our world with scores of precisely calibrated factors to support life in all its abundance.

While astrophysicists claim the earth is a microscopic speck of dust in the universe, earth scientists say this planet is home to potentially millions of species, each populated by billions of representatives. By some estimates, earth's life forms include 3 trillion trees, 3.5 trillion fish, 1.5 billion cattle, 900 million dogs, and 300 million common starlings. Add in bugs and microscopic organisms, and the total soars into quadrillions.

Remarkably, scientists almost universally admit they have identified only a fraction of the life forms on earth. Despite centuries of exploration, no scientist had ever observed a spade-toothed whale until this past decade.

Imagine a mind vast enough to conceive all those living things—and a will powerful enough to bring them into being. We'll never be able to understand God—but we can draw on His power by simple trust.

GOD RULES OVER ALL

And behold, a man of God came out of Judah to Bethel,
by the word of the LORD, and Jeroboam stood by the
altar to burn incense. And he cried against the altar
in the word of the LORD and said, "O altar, altar, this
is what the LORD says, 'Behold, a child shall be born
to the house of David, Josiah by name, and on you he
shall offer the priests of the high places who burn incense
on you, and men's bones shall be burned on you.'"

1 KINGS 13:1–2 SKJV

Josiah: Which being done above three hundred years after
this prophecy, plainly shews the absolute certainty of God's
providence and foreknowledge even in the most contingent
things. For this was in itself uncertain and wholly depended
upon man's will, both as to the having of a child and as to
the giving it this name. Therefore God can certainly and
effectually overrule man's will which way He pleaseth; or
else it was possible that this prediction should have been
false, which is blasphemous to imagine.

Whoever is sent on God's errand must not fear the
faces of men. It was above three hundred and fifty years ere
this prophecy was fulfilled. Yet it is spoken of as sure and
nigh at hand. For a thousand years are with God as one day.

TOO MANY WARRIORS

*The LORD said to Gideon, "You have too many
warriors with you. If I let all of you fight the
Midianites, the Israelites will boast to me that
they saved themselves by their own strength."*

JUDGES 7:2 NLT

Scripture doesn't tell us how large the army of the
Midianites was. But Judges 7:12 indicates that their camels
were "too many to count." And we know that twenty-two
thousand of Israel's thirty-two thousand soldiers were
frightened enough to gladly leave when given the opportunity (verse 3).

Even so, the Lord told Gideon that he still had too
many warriors. God eventually trimmed the number to
just three hundred, to keep Israel from boasting that their
own strength had given them victory. The tiny army's
rout of the Midianites left no doubt about God's power.

When facing challenges, our natural inclination is to
trust our own strength. We trust our retirement funds,
our good health, our solid jobs, our family and friends,
or a dozen other things. But any of those could be taken
away in an instant. The Lord wants to reduce our trust
in such stuff so we'll learn to trust Him.

Stop and think of God's faithfulness to you and your
family in the past. How has He come through for you
when you didn't stand an earthly chance? Praise the Lord
for that faithfulness—and allow those memories to deepen
your trust in Him.

WAITING ON GOD

Rest in the LORD, and wait patiently for Him. Do not fret because of him who prospers in his way, because of the man who brings wicked schemes to pass. Cease from anger, and forsake wrath. Do not fret in this way to do evil. For evildoers shall be cut off, but those who wait on the LORD, they shall inherit the earth.

PSALM 37:7–9 SKJV

"In patience possess your souls" (Luke 21:19). "Ye have need of patience" (Hebrews 10:36). "Let patience have her perfect work, that ye may be perfect and entire" (James 1:4). Such words of the Holy Spirit show us what an important element in the Christian life and character patience is. And nowhere is there a better place for cultivating or displaying it than in waiting on God.

There we discover how impatient we are and what our impatience means. We confess at times that we are impatient with men and circumstances that hinder us or with ourselves and our slow progress in the Christian life. If we truly set ourselves to wait upon God, we shall find it is with Him we are impatient because He does not at once, or as soon as we could wish, do our bidding. It is in waiting upon God that our eyes are opened to believe in His wise and sovereign will and to see that the sooner and the more completely we yield absolutely to it, the more surely His blessing can come to us.

NOTHING IS TOO HARD FOR GOD

*"Ah, Sovereign LORD, you have made the
heavens and the earth by your great power and
outstretched arm. Nothing is too hard for you."*
JEREMIAH 32:17 NIV

Jeremiah's prayer above is a beautiful statement of God's power. If you read all of chapter 32, however, you see that the prayer is followed by an implied *but*.

Throughout the previous two chapters, the Lord had promised to restore exiled Israel—in its homeland. Then God said He would make a new covenant with His people—in their hearts. After the first promise, Jeremiah said, "My sleep had been pleasant to me" (31:26 NIV). After the second, Jeremiah stopped dictating to his assistant, Baruch. They must have rejoiced at these wonderful promises.

But then we come to Jeremiah 32, where the Babylonians are ready to overrun Jerusalem. Jeremiah is imprisoned by the wicked king of Judah. And God has commanded him to buy property in his hometown (verses 6–8)!

In response to this command, Jeremiah praised the Lord's omnipotence (verses 17, 21), then complained about spending money on land he never expected to use. In reply, God told Jeremiah, "I am the LORD, the God of all mankind. Is anything too hard for me?" (verse 27 NIV). He went on to explain that the Babylonians were fulfilling His own plans for His people.

Though they were being disciplined, they were always God's beloved people—a nation that He promised to restore and bless. Through Jesus, God does the same thing for us as Christians today.

DWELLING IN ANOTHER COUNTRY

". . .a land that the LORD your God cares for.
The eyes of the LORD your God are always on it,
from the beginning of the year to the end of the year."
DEUTERONOMY 11:12 SKJV

Observe here a type of the condition of the natural and the spiritual man. In this world in temporals and in all other respects the merely carnal man has to be his own providence and to look to himself for all his needs. Hence his cares are always many, and frequently they become so heavy that they drive him to desperation. He lives a life of care, anxiety, sorrow, fretfulness and disappointment.

But the spiritual man dwells in another country; his faith makes him a citizen of another land. It is true he endures the same toils and experiences the same afflictions as the ungodly, but they deal with him after another fashion, for they come as a gracious Father's appointments, and they go at the bidding of loving wisdom. By faith the godly man casts his care upon God who careth for him, and he walks without carking care because he knows himself to be the child of heaven's loving-kindness, for whom all things work together for good.

God is his great guardian and friend, and all his concerns are safe in the hands of infinite grace.

STRENGTH IN NUMBERS

We are in this struggle together.
PHILIPPIANS 1:30 NLT

The great thing about challenges for the believer is that we don't struggle alone.

Christian men have two responsibilities in this arena: to confide in our brothers and to bear one another's burdens. By doing these things, we both give and receive strength.

"Confess your sins to each other and pray for each other so that you may be healed" (James 5:16 NLT). When we admit that we're struggling, whether with a particular sin or some spiritual, emotional, physical, or relational challenge, we are on our way toward finding help. Laying down our pride and confessing that we need help will allow God to do powerful work within our lives and the lives of those around us.

"Share each other's burdens, and in this way obey the law of Christ" (Galatians 6:2 NLT). Our second responsibility is to step up and help our fellows. If we see a brother struggling in any way, our responsibility is to lend a hand. This task requires us to put aside critical, negative thoughts and, in love, help our brother get back onto his feet—or, more specifically, back to Jesus.

Interestingly, we can fulfill our second responsibility even when we're struggling ourselves. Be ready to ask for help, and be ready to help, any time and every time. Always remember, as the apostle Paul said, "We are in this struggle together."

FROM THE KING'S PALACE

*Now because we receive support from the king's palace,
and it was not proper for us to see the king's dishonor,
therefore, we have sent and informed the king.*

EZRA 4:14 SKJV

There is no help for the child of God if his heavenly Father should shut the granary door. If out of the king's palace there came no portions of meat in due season, we might lay us down and die of despair. Who could hold us up but God? Who could guide us but God? Who could keep us from falling into perdition but God? Who could from hour to hour supply our desperate wants but God?

Is it not, then, right well for us—abundantly well—that we have had our maintenance from the king's palace? While we turn over this very sweet thought, we may remember that our maintenance from the king's palace has cost His Majesty dear. He has not fed us for nothing. It cost Him His own dear Son at the very first.

We should not have begun to live if He had spared His Son and kept Him back from us; but the choicest treasure in heaven He was pleased to spend for our sakes that we might live; and ever since then we have been fed upon Jesus Christ Himself.

STRANGLED BY WORRY

"Can all your worries add
a single moment to your life?"
MATTHEW 6:27 NLT

This world can be a frightening place. It's full of uncertainty, from diseases to terrorism to economic upheaval. Things often seem out of control, and we feel weak. That's where worry steps in. In a strange way, worry gives us a sense of control over situations.

The word *worry* comes from an Old English term meaning "to strangle." By worrying a situation, we are trying to get our arms around it, to subdue it. But *we* are the worried ones—the problem has its arms around us. By giving into worry, we allow ourselves to be strangled.

What should we do instead? Philippians 4:6 says, "Don't worry about anything; instead, pray about everything. Tell God what you need, and thank him for all he has done" (NLT).

While worry gives an illusion of control, prayer recognizes the God who's in control. When we put our problems in His hands, we are trusting His ability to take care of them. Pray. Commit the outcome of worrying situations to the Lord. Remember those times when God has proved Himself to be faithful.

This world can be a frightening place, but it doesn't need to be. By relinquishing our control to the Lord, we can overcome worry and be truly courageous.

GREAT IS GOD'S FAITHFULNESS

Yet this I call to mind and therefore I have
hope: Because of the LORD's great love we are not
consumed, for his compassions never fail. They are
new every morning; great is your faithfulness.
LAMENTATIONS 3:21–23 NIV

The book of Lamentations is aptly named. It contains a series of five laments written by Jeremiah after the destruction of Judah's crown jewel: Jerusalem.

These laments read like a drama, with lines given to the ravaged people's belated prayers to God (see 1:9, 1:11, 1:20–22, 2:20–22), futile cries for someone to comfort them (see 1:12–16), sorrow over their suffering children (see 2:12), and the taunts of their oppressors (see 2:16–17).

Jeremiah's own suffering can be heard throughout chapters 1 and 2, before taking center stage in chapter 3. However, a third of the way through that triple acrostic (three verses for each letter of the Hebrew alphabet), Jeremiah shines the spotlight on his enduring faith and hope in the Lord God.

If anyone had cause to lose hope—humanly speaking—it was Jeremiah. After forty years of serving the Lord, though, how could Jeremiah walk away? Centuries later, the apostle Peter said it well: "*Lord*, to whom shall we go? *You* have the words of eternal life" (John 6:68 NIV, emphasis added).

This world is broken. This life is hard. But God's faithfulness is great. He has the words—and the power—of eternal life.

THE BASICS

*"Brothers and sisters, choose seven men from among you
who are known to be full of the Spirit and wisdom. We
will turn this responsibility over to them and will give
our attention to prayer and the ministry of the word."*

ACTS 6:3–4 NIV

Believers often find themselves in tough situations. The
world, the flesh, and the devil all conspire to derail us
from our true calling. Hardships—some out of the blue,
some of our own creation—drag us down emotionally.
The apostles who spoke the words of today's verse had
just been arrested and flogged for preaching about Jesus
(Acts 5:17–42).

But even though these early Christian leaders lived
difficult lives, they knew their basic duties were simple:
praying and studying God's Word. Knowing God more
deeply and spending time in His presence were the uncom-
plicated things that provided courage for their challenges.

In Acts 6, the apostles prioritized their "quiet time"
with God over the physical duties of the church—
specifically, distributing food to the needy widows. That
decision in no way implied that the church leaders were
more important than the widows or above physical
work. . .notice that they arranged for seven wise, godly
men to oversee that distribution. But the apostles knew
they needed Bible study and prayer to best serve the
overall church with their spiritual leadership.

An old Sunday school song really captures the truth
of the Christian life: "Read your Bible, pray every day,
and you'll grow, grow, grow."

STRONGER THAN SAMSON

*Now [Samson] was suddenly very thirsty. He called out
to GOD, "You have given your servant this great victory.
Are you going to abandon me to die of thirst and fall into
the hands of the uncircumcised?" So God split open the
rock basin in Lehi; water gushed out and Samson drank.*

JUDGES 15:18–19 MSG

After taking out a group of Philistine soldiers with a make-
shift weapon, Samson sang a brief song: "With a donkey's
jawbone I made heaps of donkeys of them. With a donkey's
jawbone I killed an entire company" (Judges 15:16 MSG).
Then he realized he was thirsty, which may have been an
aspect of God's discipline on the willful judge of Israel.

Samson's thirst was "a natural effect of the great pains
he had taken," John Wesley wrote. "And perhaps there was
the hand of God therein, to chastise him for not making
mention of God in his song, and to keep him from being
proud of his strength."

Even Samson's prayer above has an edge to it. He
seemed exasperated by his thirst and God's "abandonment"
of him. In His mercy, God miraculously provided water.

That's the amazing thing about God: He often blesses
us with good things even when we fail Him—when our
hearts are cold and distracted, when we've consciously
chosen to sin. Let's be sure to acknowledge His blessings,
but also to root out the attitudes and actions that separate us from God. If we can consistently do that, we'll be
stronger than Samson ever was.

WAIT ON THE LORD

*I say to myself, "The L*ORD *is my portion; therefore I*
*will wait for him." The L*ORD *is good to those whose*
hope is in him, to the one who seeks him; it is good
*to wait quietly for the salvation of the L*ORD.
LAMENTATIONS 3:24–26 NIV

In today's scripture, Jeremiah makes a pair of statements
with strong allusions to biblical history.

The first evokes imagery from Joshua 13–21. The
earlier chapters of Joshua are all about conquest, but this
latter part of the book concerns "portions." One tribe
of Israel at a time was assigned its own portion of the
promised land. Each portion was mapped and described
in detail. You can imagine the people's excitement:
"This is what we've been waiting for! Our portion of the
promised land!" Sadly, before long the people forgot
that their infinite, eternal portion was the Lord God
Himself (see also Psalm 16:5, 73:26, 119:57, and 142:5).

Jeremiah's second statement evokes imagery from
Genesis 12–24. Throughout these chapters, Abraham—the
father of faith in the Lord God—did exactly what Jeremiah
described. That is, Abraham hoped in the Lord, sought
Him, and waited quietly for His salvation.

Abraham's faith, it turns out, is a model for all of us.
The apostle Paul wrote, "Against all hope, Abraham in
hope believed and so became the father of many nations"
(Romans 4:18 NIV). Jesus Himself said, "Abraham rejoiced
at the thought of seeing my day; he saw it and was glad"
(John 8:56 NIV).

Wait on the Lord. He will provide exactly what you
need, at exactly the right moment.

WE OWE OUR SUCCESSES TO THE LORD

And the priest gave to the captains over hundreds King David's spears and shields that were in the temple of the LORD.

2 KINGS 11:10 SKJV

Every genuine Christian has to fight. Every inch of the way between here and heaven we shall have to fight, for as hitherto every single step of our pilgrimage has been one prolonged conflict. Sometimes we have victories, a presage of that final victory, that perfect triumph we shall enjoy with our Great Captain forever.

When we have these victories it behooves us to be especially careful that in all good conscience we hang up the trophies thereof in the house of the Lord. The reason for this lies here: it is to the Lord that we owe any success we have ever achieved. We have been defeated when we have gone in our own strength; but when we have been victorious it has always been because the strength of the Lord was put forth for our deliverance.

GOD WILL PROVIDE

Isaac spoke up and said to his father Abraham,
"Father?" "Yes, my son?" Abraham replied. "The fire
and wood are here," Isaac said, "but where is the lamb
for the burnt offering?" Abraham answered, "God
himself will provide the lamb for the burnt offering,
my son." And the two of them went on together.

GENESIS 22:7–8 NIV

This almost incomprehensible request for Abraham to take Isaac to the distant mountains and offer him as a sacrifice had two possible outcomes. Either Abraham would prove his love for God by slaughtering his son on an altar, or God would somehow provide an alternative. Abraham knew that God would provide.

As believers, we often face situations in which the outcome is uncertain. But when seemingly impossible choices are all we see, we can act in confident faith, following the example of Abraham.

Centuries after this incident, the New Testament writer James said, "And the scripture was fulfilled that says, 'Abraham believed God, and it was credited to him as righteousness,' and he was called God's friend" (James 2:23 NIV). In this moment of extreme challenge, Abraham trusted his long-established friendship with God. He approached his terrible task in faith—and God did provide an alternative (see Genesis 22:12–13).

Along the path of life, our simple acts of obedience to God accumulate. And, like Abraham when the crisis comes, we find that trusting God is not only possible. It's the best possible option.

NO SCHEMING NECESSARY

"The LORD bless you, my daughter," [Boaz] replied
[to Ruth]. "This kindness is greater than that
which you showed earlier: You have not run after
the younger men, whether rich or poor."

RUTH 3:10 NIV

The first time he saw her, it seems Boaz was taken with Ruth (Ruth 2:5). Most likely considerably older, Boaz went out of his way to accommodate Ruth—and warning his men not to lay a hand on her. Imagine his surprise when he went to sleep in the threshing floor one night and woke up to find Ruth lying at his feet! She informed Boaz that he was her guardian-redeemer.

It would have been easy for Boaz to make Ruth his wife right away. Scripture doesn't say whether he was tempted to do so, but we do see his impressive actions. Knowing he wasn't the nearest guardian-redeemer, Boaz invited the other man to step in, then trusted God for the results. You probably know the rest of the story: the closer relative said "no," so Boaz ended up marrying Ruth.

Boaz and Ruth both acted honorably, exhibiting high moral character and a humble reliance on God when it would have been easy to act on impulse. We know—from the Bible and from personal experience—that God provides exactly what we need, when we need it. Remember that truth and trust Him to take care of you. He'll often provide what you want as well.

CLEAR PROOF OF GOD'S LOVE

*"Can a virgin forget her accessories,
or a bride her attire? Yet My people have
forgotten Me days without number."*

JEREMIAH 2:32 SKJV

It is a clear proof of the great love of God to His people that He will not lose their love without earnest expostulation. When you do not care at all for a person, he may love you or hate you, it is all the same to you; but when you have great love for him, then you earnestly desire to possess his heart in return. This, then, is clear proof that God greatly loves His people, since, whenever their hearts wander from Him, He is greatly grieved, and He rebukes them and earnestly pleads with them setting the coldness of their hearts in a true light and striving to bring them back to warm affection towards Himself.

Not only are God's rebukes proofs of His love, but when He goes farther and deals out blows as well as words, there is love in every stroke of His hand. Most truly does He say, "As many as I love I rebuke and chasten" (Revelation 3:19), since rebukes and chastenings are proofs that He will not lose our hearts without a struggle for them.

A NEW HEART

*"I [God] will give [the returning exiled Israelites] an
undivided heart and put a new spirit in them; I will
remove from them their heart of stone and give them
a heart of flesh. Then they will follow my decrees and
be careful to keep my laws. They will be my people,
and I will be their God. . . . I will give you a new
heart and put a new spirit in you; I will remove from
you your heart of stone and give you a heart of flesh.
And I will put my Spirit in you and move you to
follow my decrees and be careful to keep my laws."*

EZEKIEL 11:19–20; 36:26–27 NIV

Throughout Ezekiel's ministry, the Lord spoke of His rebellious people having hardened hearts of stone. The imagery suggests a catastrophic stroke, paralysis, and impending death (think of the demise of Nabal in 1 Samuel 25:37). More importantly, it suggests an irrational, pride-induced, resolute refusal to obey the Lord, no matter how severe the consequences (think of the Pharaoh in Exodus 4:21–14:8).

Yet the Lord offered to give them (and, by extension, *us*) the best possible exchange: a new heart of flesh filled with His Spirit. Then God's people can obey Him willingly, regularly, gladly.

What could provide more courage than a living, passionate heart for God? He will provide it as we ask.

NOT FORGOTTEN

"I have also acquired Ruth the Moabite, Mahlon's widow, as my wife, in order to maintain the name of the dead with his property, so that his name will not disappear from among his family or from his hometown. Today you are witnesses!"

Ruth 4:10 niv

Naomi returned to Bethlehem a broken woman. She'd lost her husband, Elimelech, and her two sons, Mahlon and Chilion. And when Naomi appeared in Bethlehem with her daughter-in-law Ruth, her former neighbors weren't even sure who she was (Ruth 1:19–20). She no longer wanted to be called Naomi (meaning "beautiful" or "pleasant"), but rather Mara ("bitter"). She had lost much, and she was bitter. Worst of all, Naomi felt like God had abandoned her.

Of course, God was still with Naomi. And so was Ruth. And eventually, a guardian-redeemer in the form of Boaz. He gathered the leaders and the people together and made the proclamation you read in today's verse. Naomi's son Mahlon would not be forgotten. Neither would Naomi herself, as she would become the grandmother of Ruth's son Obed, who would have a son named Jesse, who would father David. . .whose line eventually gave us Jesus, the Redeemer of humankind.

What have you lost? A career? A business? Your wife? Your health? A dream? God is able to touch your deepest pain and redeem it. He may restore what you've lost, or He may have other plans. Either way, He hasn't forgotten you.

REJOICE IN THE LORD

Whatever happens, my dear brothers and sisters,
rejoice in the Lord. I never get tired of telling you
these things, and I do it to safeguard your faith.
PHILIPPIANS 3:1 NLT

How are you supposed to find joy in a bad medical diagnosis? Or when a financial crisis has you scrambling? Or when an important relationship is ailing? Or when any other aspect of life is out of whack?

Rejoicing in these moments is not an easy thing. But the apostle Paul commands it. (By the way, he was in prison when he wrote those words.)

Granted, the "how" of rejoicing in the Lord is easier said than it is done. We must simply trust. Rather than questioning God's motives or the process He's ordained, just trust His plan. Allow God to take full control of the situation.

Later in the letter to the Philippians, Paul wrote, "Don't worry about anything; instead, pray about everything. Tell God what you need, and thank Him for all He has done. Then you will experience God's peace, which exceeds anything we can understand" (4:6–7 NLT). These are very practical words. When worry arises, pray. Tell God what you need. Thank Him for His faithful provision already. And wait for His peace.

In our darkest moments, Jesus shines brightest. Rejoice in the Lord always, no matter what.

NO CONTEST

*The chariots of God are tens of thousands
and thousands of thousands.*

PSALM 68:17 NIV

In the Old Testament, chariots were often the measure of an army's strength. When pursuing the Israelites fleeing their slavery in Egypt, Pharaoh sent "six hundred of the best chariots, along with all the other chariots of Egypt" (Exodus 14:7 NIV). Pagan kings opposing the Israelites' entry into the promised land "came out with all their troops and a large number of horses and chariots—a huge army" (Joshua 11:4 NIV). Philistines in King Saul's day massed against Israel with "three thousand chariots, six thousand charioteers, and soldiers as numerous as the sand on the seashore" (1 Samuel 13:5 NIV).

Guess what? In each case, the Israelites prevailed. But not because of their own strength and courage—every battle was won by the Lord.

If you are God's child, it doesn't matter how many enemies line up against you. He has myriads of chariots and soldiers at His disposal. Never forget the experience of Elisha's servant. The prophet prayed, "Open his eyes, LORD, so that he may see." And God did. "The LORD opened the servant's eyes, and he looked and saw the hills full of horses and chariots of fire all around Elisha" (2 Kings 6:17 NIV). Really, it's no contest.

YOUR RESPONSIBILITY, AND NO MORE

*"The soul that sins, it shall die. The son shall not bear the
iniquity of the father, nor shall the father bear the iniquity
of the son. The righteousness of the righteous shall be on
him, and the wickedness of the wicked shall be on him."*

EZEKIEL 18:20 SKJV

Every human being sins and is guilty before God (Romans
3:23). That is the bad news that colors our entire world.
But there is good news: Every human being also has the
opportunity to accept God's free gift of salvation (John
3:16). This is a personal choice that, once made, makes us
much-loved members of God's family, with all the rights,
privileges, and protections that new relationship offers.

Sadly, not everyone makes good choices—whether
in the ultimate decision to receive Jesus or the day-by-
day behaviors that define our lives. Poor choices by the
people we love can create tension in our own lives, but
the prophet Ezekiel offers peace and strength in the words
of God Himself: each person is individually responsible.

Your father's choices, good or bad, won't pick you up
or tear you down in God's eyes (Ezekiel 18:14–18). Your
children's choices, good or bad, won't help or hurt you
before God either (verses 5–13). When you live a faithful
Christian life, God accepts that as your "reasonable service"
(Romans 12:1 SKJV).

Definitely pray for your loved ones who make poor
choices, and try to point them to God's better way. But
don't take on more responsibility than God assigns. "The
righteousness of the righteous" (*Jesus'* righteousness) will
be on you.

STAND LIKE A KING

*And it came to pass, when Ahab saw Elijah,
that Ahab said to him, "Are you he who troubles
Israel?" And he answered, "I have not troubled Israel,
but you and your father's house have, in that you have
forsaken the commandments of the LORD and you have
followed the Baals. Now therefore, send and gather to
me all Israel to Mount Carmel, and the four hundred
and fifty prophets of Baal and the four hundred
prophets of Asherah who eat at Jezebel's table."*

1 KINGS 18:17–19 SKJV

When Elijah stood on Mount Carmel, Ahab did not see who was with him. Little did he know the prophet's God; little did he think that, when Elijah walked up Mount Carmel, God walked with him. Talk of an Alexander making the world tremble at the tread of his armies!—of the marches and victories of a Caesar, or a Napoleon! The man who is walking with God is greater than all the Caesars and Napoleons and Alexanders who ever lived. Little did Ahab and the false prophets of Baal know that Elijah was walking with the same God with whom Enoch walked before the flood. Elijah was nothing when out of communion with God; but when walking in the power of God, he stood on Mount Carmel like a king.

HOLD ON

So Jacob was left alone, and a man wrestled with him till daybreak. When the man saw that he could not overpower him, he touched the socket of Jacob's hip so that his hip was wrenched as he wrestled with the man. Then the man said, "Let me go, for it is daybreak." But Jacob replied, "I will not let you go unless you bless me."
GENESIS 32:24–26 NIV

Jacob was dreading the morning. He would come face-to-face with his twin brother, Esau, the man he had cheated nearly twenty years earlier. Jacob was obeying God's instruction to return to his homeland, but he was full of anxiety about the next day.

Apparently unable to sleep, Jacob prayed for God's protection. Then he went off alone to plot ways of appeasing Esau, to "pacify him with these gifts I am sending on ahead" (Genesis 32:20 NIV).

Late in the night, a mysterious "man" confronted Jacob. Hours of exhausting wrestling followed, but neither Jacob nor his opponent was able to prevail. As daybreak arrived, this angel of God, who Jacob identified later as God Himself (see Genesis 32:30), tried to disengage and leave. But Jacob held on longer, insisting on a blessing.

He had learned, after years of relying on his own strength and cunning, that all he truly needed to face Esau was the blessing of God. Jacob held tightly to the Lord, understanding what would later be written in Psalm 55:22: "Cast your cares on the LORD and he will sustain you; he will never let the righteous be shaken" (NIV).

THE FIRST OPTION: PRAYER

[Hannah] said to him, "Pardon me, my lord. As surely
as you live, I am the woman who stood here beside
you praying to the LORD. I prayed for this child, and
the LORD has granted me what I asked of him.

1 SAMUEL 1:26–27 NIV

Yes, this is a "girl's story" in a men's devotional book. But the account of God answering Hannah's desperate prayer for a son carries a powerful lesson for everyone.

Hannah was one of Elkanah's two wives. That fact alone would create difficulties for the barren Hannah. But life was especially hard because the other wife, Peninnah, had children. And she seemed to take pleasure in reminding Hannah of their differing motherhood status.

Elkanah seemed to love Hannah but offered only clumsy comments like, "Don't I mean more to you than ten sons?" (1 Samuel 1:8 NIV). At Israel's worship center at Shiloh, the priest Eli initially thought Hannah's anguished, wordless praying was drunkenness (verse 14). When she explained, Eli wisely reconsidered, and said, "May the God of Israel grant you what you have asked of him" (verse 17 NIV).

And God did. Hannah ultimately gave birth to a baby named Samuel, who would become one of Israel's great leaders. But that would likely not have happened apart from her prayers.

Today, we have the same opportunity to pray that Hannah had—and took full advantage of. Prayer should never be a last resort, but a first option. It's the quickest and most effective way to tap into God's strength for our daily challenges.

ARE YOU OUT OF YOUR MIND?

When his family heard what was happening,
they tried to take him away. "He's
out of his mind," they said.

MARK 3:21 NLT

Near the beginning of Jesus' ministry, word traveled from Capernaum—where Jesus was healing the sick and casting out demons—to his hometown of Nazareth about twenty miles away. His family heard the reports of the miracle-working rabbi who consorted with tax collectors. They determined that Jesus had gone crazy.

As loving family members, they made the twenty-mile trip to Capernaum to bring Him home. They wanted to talk some sense into Jesus. When a disciple told Jesus that His mother and brothers were outside, He replied, "Who is my mother? Who are my brothers?" Then He looked around and said, "Look, these are my mother and brothers. Anyone who does God's will is my brother and sister and mother" (Mark 3:33–35 NLT).

That wasn't going to calm His family's fears.

The reality is that following Jesus—doing what He tells us to do and seeking His Father's will more than the approval of the world—may make us seem insane. But that's okay.

Our courage does not come from the world's approval. Doing God's will makes us strong. Our family and friends may not understand what we're doing. That's okay too. In time, like Jesus' own brothers, they may come around. The important thing is that we always do what God wants first.

There's nothing crazy about that.

THE RECORD OF MERCY

You drew near on the day that I called
on You. You said, "Do not fear."
LAMENTATIONS 3:57 SKJV

Brethren, if our experiences have so far exceeded our expectations and belied our doubts, let us take care that we record them. Do not let us suffer our lamentations to be written in a book, and our thanksgivings to be spoken to the wind. Write not your complaints in marble and your praises upon the sand. Let the record of mercy received be carefully made, accurately measured, distinctly worded, correctly dated and so preserved that in years to come you may turn for your encouragement to it.

Jeremiah tells us that on such a day the Lord drew near to him; David remembered God from the Hermons and the hill Mizar; time and place are elements of interest in the memory of the Lord's great goodness. Note the particulars, dwell on the details—abundantly utter the memory of the divine loving-kindness.

COMMITTED TO GOD, NO MATTER WHAT

"If we are thrown into the blazing furnace, the God we serve is able to deliver us from it, and he will deliver us from Your Majesty's hand. But even if he does not, we want you to know, Your Majesty, that we will not serve your gods or worship the image of gold you have set up."

DANIEL 3:17–18 NIV

The undisputed king of the world's first great superpower, Nebuchadnezzar, was a tyrant. He didn't hesitate to order an instant death for anyone who displeased him. Few men even wanted to be in his presence.

On the other hand, at the end of Daniel 2, "the king appointed Shadrach, Meshach and Abednego administrators over the province of Babylon" *at Daniel's request* (verse 49 NIV). Up to this point, Daniel's friends had done nothing but please Nebuchadnezzar.

How quickly one's circumstances and station in life can change! Yet the more the king threatened them, the more Daniel's friends resolutely insisted they would serve and worship only the one true God.

You probably know how the story ends: a furious Nebuchadnezzar had Shadrach, Meshach, and Abednego thrown into a blazing furnace. But God brought them through the fire without a singed hair or even a smell of smoke. The Lord proved His absolute superiority to even the world's strongest, most frightening ruler.

When you commit to God no matter what, He will also take care of you—bringing you through the fire or taking you on to heaven. Christians really can't lose.

GOD ALWAYS HAS A PLAN

*On that day a great persecution broke out against
the church in Jerusalem, and all except the apostles
were scattered throughout Judea and Samaria.
Godly men buried Stephen and mourned deeply for
him. But Saul began to destroy the church. Going
from house to house, he dragged off both men and
women and put them in prison. Those who had been
scattered preached the word wherever they went.*

ACTS 8:1–4 NIV

After the Holy Spirit arrived at Pentecost, it was time
for the disciples to go into "all the world" to preach the
good news about Jesus. They met opposition everywhere,
culminating in the stoning of Stephen.

If that was where the story of Acts stopped, we might
question God's plan. After all, if *we* were writing a script for
the start of the church, we would probably have included
a lot less persecution.

But we don't write our own stories—not entirely. We
can't fully control our own future. At some point, we will
find ourselves in hard situations, difficulties similar to those
early believers up in the drama of first-century Jerusalem.

Thankfully, though, God always has a plan. And in
Acts 8:4, we see what it was: to spread the good news of
Jesus throughout the Roman world and beyond. As you
continue to read through Acts, you'll see that He even
planned to use Saul, the chief persecutor.

We don't always know what God has in store for our
lives. But we can be sure that *He* does, and that His plans
are for our best.

WHO CAN STAND?

*And the people of Beth Shemesh asked,
"Who can stand in the presence of
the LORD, this holy God?"*

1 SAMUEL 6:20 NIV

You probably already know that Old Testament Israel committed many sins. Did you know they almost made an idol of the ark of the covenant?

The ark was the single point where God would meet with the people through their high priest—but the Israelites began to view it as a kind of good-luck charm. They foolishly took the ark into battle against the Philistines and lost it to their archenemies.

After the Philistines suffered from the ark's presence, they were happy to send it back to Israel on a cart pulled by two cows. But at Beth Shemesh, where the cows stopped, the people's joy turned to horror when God struck down seventy of them for looking inside the ark. The townspeople then asked the questions you see in today's verse. They were at a loss as to how to approach a holy God.

Even today, we may try to approach God through rituals or a moral code—but our sin nature always causes us to fall short. We can never be good enough for God. But there is good news: we can come to God on the basis of Jesus Christ's righteousness.

If your spiritual life ever grows dry, or if you feel distant from God due to a self-inflicted hardship, don't make the same mistake Israel made. Throw yourself at the foot of the cross in humble repentance. Allow the righteousness of Christ to bring you close to the Father.

GROW YOUR ROOTS

*Let your roots grow down into him, and let
your lives be built on him. Then your faith
will grow strong in the truth you were taught.*

COLOSSIANS 2:7 NLT

Without its roots, a tree would be unable to draw water from the ground for its life and health. Without roots, trees would topple over at the first strong gust of wind. For these reasons, God made a tree's roots to grow deep and wide.

The apostle Paul used roots as a word picture for our Christian growth. "Let your roots grow down into him," Paul said, referring to Christ Jesus your Lord (see verse 6). "Let your lives be built on him." And then what? "Your faith will grow strong in the truth you were taught."

What truth were you taught? The basic doctrines—of creation, sin, Christ, and salvation. The truth of scripture, from which we learn everything we need for godly living.

When our roots go deep into God's Word, we find living water. We are nourished and strengthened for whatever comes our way, including the storms of life. We'll be able to withstand even the pummeling winds of a spiritual hurricane.

Second Timothy 3:14–16 tells us that God uses His Word to teach us, to grow us, and to equip us to live well for Him. Commit to reading the Word regularly, as well as studying and memorizing it. Let your roots grow deep into scripture, so you can find courage for life.

GOD IS STILL WORKING

Then Samuel took a stone and set it between Mizpah and Shen and called it Ebenezer, saying, "Up to this point the LORD has helped us."
1 SAMUEL 7:12 SKJV

It is certainly a very delightful thing to mark the hand of God in the lives of ancient saints. How profitable an occupation to observe God's goodness in delivering David out of the jaw of the lion and the paw of the bear; His mercy in passing by the transgression, iniquity and sin of Manasseh; His faithfulness in keeping the covenant made with Abraham; or His interposition on the behalf of the dying Hezekiah.

But, beloved, would it not be even more interesting and profitable for us to mark the hand of God in our own lives? Ought we not to look upon our own history as being at least as full of God, as full of His goodness and His truth, as much a proof of His faithfulness and veracity as the lives of any of the saints who have gone before?

I think we do our Lord an injustice when we suppose that He wrought all His mighty acts in days of yore and showed Himself strong for those in the early time, but doth not perform wonders or lay bare His arm for the saints that are now upon the earth.

STRONGER THAN THE STRONGEST

*I, Nebuchadnezzar, raised my eyes toward heaven,
and my sanity was restored. Then I praised the Most
High; I honored and glorified him who lives forever.
His dominion is an eternal dominion; his kingdom
endures from generation to generation. . . . Now I,
Nebuchadnezzar, praise and exalt and glorify the King of
heaven, because everything he does is right and all his ways
are just. And those who walk in pride he is able to humble.*

DANIEL 4:34, 37 NIV

Today's verse is the end of the story of Nebuchadnezzar.
The powerful, prideful king of Babylon had brought God's
judgment upon himself by some ill-advised self-glory and
had spent seven years in a state of insanity, living with
wild animals and eating grass like an ox. But the Lord
was gracious to restore the king's mind, and the last time
we hear of Nebuchadnezzar in scripture, he is speaking
God's praise to his kingdom and beyond.

Two generations later, Darius the Mede made a similar statement of praise to God, sending it to the people
of every race and nation and language throughout his
empire, which comprised at least 120 provinces (Daniel
6:25–27). And a third powerful biblical king, Cyrus the
Great, issued his own statement in praise to the Lord,
the God of heaven, throughout the provinces as well (2
Chronicles 36:22–23; Ezra 1:1–4).

These men, powerful as they might have been, were
nothing in comparison to the one true God. In His hand,
"the king's heart is a stream of water that he channels
toward all who please him" (Proverbs 21:1 NIV).

And, Christian, He is on *your* side.

GOD CAN HEAR EVERY PRAYER

"If My people who are called by My name shall humble themselves and pray and seek My face and turn from their wicked ways, then I will hear from heaven and will forgive their sin and will heal their land."

2 CHRONICLES 7:14 SKJV

God has a home, and heaven is His dwelling place. How far away that home of God, that heaven, is I do not know. But one thing I do know; it is not so far away but God can hear us when we pray.

God can hear every prayer that goes up to Him there from this sin-cursed earth. We are not so far from Him but that He can see our tears and hear the faintest whisper when we lift our hearts to Him in prayer. Do we not read, "If My people, which are called by My name, shall humble themselves, and pray, and seek My face, and turn from their wicked ways, then will I hear from heaven, and will forgive their sin, and will heal their land." That is God's own word: "I will hear from heaven," and "I will forgive their sin."

GOD IS IN CONTROL

Jacob looked up and there was Esau, coming with
his four hundred men. . . . He himself went on
ahead and bowed down to the ground seven times
as he approached his brother. But Esau ran to
meet Jacob and embraced him; he threw his arms
around his neck and kissed him. And they wept.

GENESIS 33:1, 3–4 NIV

Jacob had a penchant for trusting only himself, a history of deceiving those closest to him rather than relying on God to meet his needs. But now Jacob was forced to encounter one of those he had cheated.

Jacob knew he had God's blessing. He knew he had God's favor. Still, God did not yet have Jacob's full and complete trust. Didn't he realize that God in His power could cool the anger and resentment his older brother, Esau, felt over the family blessing Jacob had stolen?

Like many of us, Jacob struggled to believe that the Lord controls the future. But He does. Centuries later, God would say to Jacob's descendants, "'I know the plans I have for you,' declares the LORD, 'plans to prosper you and not to harm you, plans to give you hope and a future'" (Jeremiah 29:11 NIV).

Jacob's positive encounter with Esau still did not convince him to fully trust God. . .but hopefully it will convince us today. God is in control of tomorrow. Trust Him to do the right thing.

GOD EMPOWERS

*Saul replied, "But I'm only from the tribe of
Benjamin, the smallest tribe in Israel, and my
family is the least important of all the families of
that tribe! Why are you talking like this to me?"*

1 SAMUEL 9:21 NLT

Saul's father, Kish, was a wealthy, influential man. And
Saul was known for being the most handsome male in
Israel (1 Samuel 9:1–2). But when he considered his
tribe's heritage—they were the smallest tribe in Israel after
being decimated in a civil war (Judges 20)—he couldn't
understand why Samuel said Saul and his family were "the
focus of all Israel's hopes" (1 Samuel 9:20).

We aren't told why Saul considered his family to
be the least important in his small tribe. Maybe he was
naturally humble. Maybe he was overwhelmed to think
that his nation's hopes would fall on his shoulders. At this
point, Saul didn't seem to understand that God was behind
him—and that after Samuel anointed him as king, God
would give Saul a new heart (1 Samuel 10:9).

The time may come when *you* are approached with
an opportunity to serve. Will you respond like Saul, with
a laundry list of reasons why you aren't able? Or will you
consider the possibility that God is leading you into a new
ministry? If the latter, be sure of this: God will empower
you to perform the job.

SUFFERING AND PERSEVERANCE

"Whoever has will be given more;
whoever does not have, even what
they have will be taken from them."

MARK 4:25 NIV

Out of context, today's verse seems not only unfair but cruel. Why give to the one who already has something? Why take from the one who doesn't? But this verse isn't referring to money or goods. It's talking about something far more precious: perseverance.

In the parable of the sower, Jesus told His listeners what happens when God's Word falls on shallow hearts. Belief sprouts easily but falls away as soon as suffering comes. In contrast, when God's Word falls on well-tilled soil, it produces a crop many times larger than what was planted.

So how do we get from shallow ground to well-tilled soil? The simple—but not easy—answer is *suffering*. Perseverance through suffering is the thing that allows God's Word in our lives to be active and growing instead of stunted and dead.

If we have perseverance, God will add understanding to our suffering and grow in us the fruits of the spirit. If we don't persevere through suffering, we are likely to walk away from our faith, casting doubt on God's faithfulness when *we* were the ones who refused to let Him till our soil properly.

The apostle Paul elaborated in Romans 5:3: "Not only so, but we also glory in our sufferings, because we know that suffering produces perseverance" (NIV).

GOD EXALTS THE HUMBLE

At Belshazzar's command, Daniel was clothed in purple,
a gold chain was placed around his neck, and he was
proclaimed the third highest ruler in the kingdom.
DANIEL 5:29 NIV

During a lengthy absence of King Nabonidus, his eldest son, Belshazzar, served as coregent over the Babylonian empire. At his command, Daniel was made "the third highest ruler in the kingdom" the very night the capital fell without a battle to Darius the Mede.

Belshazzar was killed, and one could have reasonably expected the same fate for Daniel, who had originally worked for Babylon's King Nebuchadnezzar. Instead, "It pleased Darius to appoint 120 satraps to rule throughout the kingdom, with three administrators over them, one of whom was Daniel" (6:1–2 NIV). This means that—for nearly seventy years—Daniel directly served the most powerful conquerors the world had ever known. What was his secret?

First, Daniel never compromised his faith in the one true Lord, the maker of heaven and earth, whose power dwarfs the entire universe. In comparison, who is man?

Second, Daniel never traded his humility for pride, despite every human temptation to do so. He and his three friends had it all, including good looks and sharp minds (see 1:4). Nebuchadnezzar had judged them ten times better than anyone else who served him (see 1:18–20).

Humble faith gives us courage. When we know we serve the almighty God—and that we are not Him!—there's no limit to what He can do through us.

Think about it: people are *still* talking about Daniel.

ARE YOU SURE, LORD?

The Lord told him, "Go to the house of Judas on Straight Street and ask for a man from Tarsus named Saul, for he is praying. In a vision he has seen a man named Ananias come and place his hands on him to restore his sight."

ACTS 9:11–12 NIV

The message Ananias received made no sense at all: Go and find *Saul*, the man who almost single-handedly chased the church from Jerusalem? Tell that violent persecutor about Jesus? This sounded less like God's direction and more like a trap. But when Jesus told Ananias a second time, he trusted the Lord and went.

That may seem easier said than done. Ananias was originally fearful, responding to Jesus' request by saying, "Lord. . .I have heard many reports about this man and all the harm he has done to your holy people in Jerusalem. And he has come here with authority from the chief priests to arrest all who call on your name" (verses 13–14 NIV).

But Jesus reminded Ananias (as He reminds all of us) that God's plans are good. Saul was His "chosen instrument to proclaim my name to the Gentiles" (verse 15 NIV). With this truth in mind, Ananias summoned his courage and did his job—confirming a conversion that would literally change the world.

There will be times when doing the right thing seems frightening, when we want to say, "Are You sure, Lord?" But remember His faithfulness in the past. Study His promises in scripture. And then just step out in obedience. He'll take care of you the way He took care of Ananias.

THE POWER OF THE SPIRIT

When Saul heard their words, the Spirit of God came
powerfully upon him, and he burned with anger.
1 SAMUEL 11:6 NIV

After Saul was anointed king, Ammonites surrounded the Israelite city of Jabesh-gilead, causing great fear among the residents. They quickly offered to serve King Nahash, but he wanted to humiliate them by putting out their right eyes. The people asked for a week to solicit help from elsewhere in Israel.

Nahash may have believed that Jabesh-gilead was ripe for the taking, given that Israel had a new king. Saul, who early in his rule was still farming, returned from the field to learn of Jabesh-gilead's predicament. Then the Spirit of God came upon Saul with power, allowing him to lead Israel to victory.

As born-again Christians, we don't have to wait for the Spirit to come upon us. The Holy Spirit already lives inside us! What or who is your spiritual equivalent to King Nahash and the Ammonites? Is it a sin you've never been able to conquer, one that threatens to bring you down? Or is it perhaps a coworker or a neighbor or even a family member who knows how to push all your buttons? Is it laziness or workaholism or irritability or some other difficult character trait?

The answer is God's Spirit. Allow Him to prompt and empower your next steps. He will lead you to spiritual victory.

"COME UP HITHER"

One thing I have asked of the LORD, that I will seek after:
that I may dwell in the house of the LORD all the days of
my life, to behold the beauty of the LORD and to inquire
in His temple. For in the time of trouble He shall hide
me in His pavilion, in the secret of His tabernacle He
shall hide me. He shall set me up on a rock. And now
my head shall be lifted up above my enemies around
me. Therefore I will offer in His tabernacle sacrifices of
joy. I will sing, yes, I will sing praises to the LORD.
PSALM 27:4–6 SKJV

One glimpse of Christ will pay us for all we are called upon to endure here—to see the King in His beauty, to be in the presence of the King! And then, oh! The sweet thought, we shall be like Him when we see Him! And we shall see Him in His beauty; we shall see Him high and exalted. When He was down here on earth it was the time of His humiliation, when He was cast out from the world, spit upon and rejected; but God hath exalted Him and put Him at the right hand of power, and there He is now, and there we shall see Him by and by.

A few more tears, a few more shadows, and then the voice of God shall say, "Come up hither," and into the presence of the King we shall go.

SEEING THE EXALTED LORD

*"In my vision at night I looked, and there before me
was one like a son of man, coming with the clouds
of heaven. He approached the Ancient of Days and
was led into his presence. He was given authority,
glory and sovereign power; all nations and peoples of
every language worshiped him. His dominion is an
everlasting dominion that will not pass away, and
his kingdom is one that will never be destroyed."*

DANIEL 7:13–14 NIV

Isaiah, Jeremiah, Ezekiel, and Daniel didn't just receive verbal revelations from the Lord God. They each also had stunning visions of Him, on earth (sometimes with cherubs), in the air (often with clouds), and in heaven (usually with God's throne center stage).

In the vision related in today's reading, Daniel sees "coming with the clouds of heaven" one who is clearly divine yet called "a son of man." Eternal, infinitely powerful, and worshipped by "all nations and peoples of every language," this mysterious person is revealed by the New Testament.

Throughout the Gospels, Jesus calls Himself "the Son of Man" dozens of times. In the book of Acts, after Jesus' resurrection and ascension, Luke describes the martyrdom of Stephen, who "looked up to heaven and saw the glory of God, and Jesus standing at the right hand of God. 'Look,' he said, 'I see heaven open and the Son of Man standing at the right hand of God'" (Acts 7:55–56 NIV).

How do you see Jesus? The more awesome He is to you, the more He can do in your life.

A PROPER RESPONSE

*Now Israel loved Joseph more than any of his other sons,
because he had been born to him in his old age; and he
made an ornate robe for him. When his brothers saw
that their father loved him more than any of them, they
hated him and could not speak a kind word to him.*

GENESIS 37:3–4 NIV

Family dynamics, when handled poorly, can create a myriad
of problems. Israel (formerly known as Jacob) fathered
more than a dozen children by four different women, and
he chose to show extreme favoritism to one. It was not a
formula for a happy home.

Joseph, as the oldest son of Israel's favored wife, was
more highly regarded than his much older half brothers.
Succeeding chapters of Genesis show Joseph as a successful
man of God, but as a seventeen-year-old, he became an
object of brotherly scorn—to the point of his being sold
into slavery!

Faced with incredible obstacles, Joseph continued to
serve God faithfully, believing that His blessing was more
important than anything this earth could provide. God
would later use Joseph to save the lives of his father and
brothers during a famine. This was only possible because
of his choices in moments of great difficulty.

How about us? Will we respond to our challenges
with the grace Joseph showed and allow God to work all
things for good? The promise is for "those who love him,
who have been called according to his purpose" (Romans
8:28 NIV).

Commit to faithful obedience and give God room to
work. He will.

WALK IN CONFIDENCE

*And Samuel said, "How can I go? If Saul hears
of it, he will kill me." And the LORD said,
"Take a heifer with you and say, 'I have
come to sacrifice to the LORD.'"*

1 SAMUEL 16:2 SKJV

Due to Saul's pride and disobedience, the Lord rejected him as king over Israel. When God instructed Samuel to find the next king within Jesse's family, the old priest was understandably concerned. Saul would have seen the selection of his successor as an act of treason and probably tried to kill Samuel. Was the fearful reaction in today's verse a weakness in Samuel's faith?

Perhaps. But if we're honest, we realize how fearful we can be too. "The best men are not perfect in their faith," wrote the old English Bible commentator Matthew Henry, discussing Samuel's situation. "Nor will fear be wholly cast out any where on this side of heaven."

God responded by telling Samuel to offer a sacrifice, perhaps as an atonement for his weakness and doubt. Whenever we face fears over God's calling, we can be thankful that He has already provided a sacrifice for our every failure in Jesus' shed blood on the cross. We can walk in the confidence of His provision.

There are times when being a Christian may cost us something. But obeying God is always far more important. By our obedience, we can contribute to the work of His kingdom, looking forward to the day when all fear is banished.

STORMY SEAS

*Jesus was in the stern, sleeping on a cushion. The disciples
woke him and said to him, "Teacher, don't you care if
we drown?" He got up, rebuked the wind and said to
the waves, "Quiet! Be still!" Then the wind died down
and it was completely calm. He said to his disciples,
"Why are you so afraid? Do you still have no faith?"*
MARK 4:38–40 NIV

The Sea of Galilee is nearly seven hundred feet below sea
level, surrounded by hills and mountains that reach more
than twenty-five hundred feet above sea level. Shaped like
an arena, it was a perfect place for Jesus to preach while
standing in a boat.

After a long day of teaching, the Lord and His disciples set sail across the sea. Jesus was so tired that He didn't
wake up when the weather turned ugly. Although the
Sea of Galilee is beautiful, it is subject to violent storms
when wind blows cold air over the heights to the warm
water below.

As the storm grew, the disciples' boat took on water.
Jesus slept on. When the terrified disciples woke Him,
Jesus rebuked the weather. . .and then His disciples.

Though this miracle was another proof of Jesus'
authority, it only happened in response to the disciples'
lack of faith. Followers of Jesus have no reason to fear any
storm, no matter how violent, when Jesus is in the boat.
Who knows what greater miracle may have occurred if
the disciples had let Jesus sleep?

Trust that the God who shaped the land and sea, who
commands the winds—and who rests in your boat—will
bring you safely through.

LOOKING TO CHRIST WITH THE EYE OF FAITH

*. . .looking to Jesus, the author and finisher of
our faith, who for the joy that was set before Him
endured the cross, despising the shame, and is
seated at the right hand of the throne of God.*
HEBREWS 12:2 SKJV

Abraham Lincoln issued a proclamation declaring the emancipation of three millions of slaves. On a certain day their chains were to fall off, and they were to be free. The proclamation was put up on the trees and fences wherever the Northern Army marched. A good many slaves could not read: but others read the proclamation, and most of them believed it; and on a certain day a glad shout went up, "We are free!" Some did not believe it and stayed with their old masters; but it did not alter the fact that they were free.

Christ, the Captain of our salvation, has proclaimed freedom to all who have faith in Him. Let us take Him at His word. Their feelings would not have made the slaves free. The power must come from the outside. Looking at ourselves will not make us free, but it is looking to Christ with the eye of faith.

OBEY WHEN AFRAID

Then Ananias went to the house and entered it.
Placing his hands on Saul, he said, "Brother Saul,
the Lord—Jesus, who appeared to you on the road
as you were coming here—has sent me so that you
may see again and be filled with the Holy Spirit."
Immediately, something like scales fell from Saul's eyes,
and he could see again. He got up and was baptized,
and after taking some food, he regained his strength.
ACTS 9:17–19 NIV

The conversion of Saul on the road to Damascus is pivotal in church history. Soon to be called Paul, the former persecutor of Christians would go on to write much of the New Testament. These books detail the victories and defeats of the early church, explain deep truths about God and Jesus, and serve as a template for godly living.

When you consider these truths, can you imagine what might have happened had Ananias given in to fear and refused the Spirit's command to visit Saul? The Christian church and our Bibles would look much different today.

The good news is that, in God's perfect plan and will, Ananias did obey—even though he was afraid. Remember, Saul was known as the destroyer of the church, a man whose actions scattered thousands of Christians throughout the Roman world.

Fear can be paralyzing. But God is in the habit of healing paralysis. When He commands, through His Word or the nudging of His Spirit, just go. God has infinite power to take care of the rest.

A NEW CALLING

So Samuel took the horn of oil and anointed him in the presence of his brothers, and from that day on the Spirit of the LORD came powerfully upon David.

1 SAMUEL 16:13 NIV

In the Middle East of the Old Testament, families often assigned the youngest boy to serve as shepherd. They would lead their sheep with a rod and staff—which David described so beautifully in Psalm 23—into places of good food and water. Shepherds were also responsible for protecting their flocks from predators.

When Samuel visited Jesse to discover which of his eight sons should be Israel's next king, David—the youngest, away with the sheep—was the last to be summoned. Apparently, Jesse believed David to be an unlikely candidate. David would probably have agreed. He was simply performing his family duty when God called him to be king. At that point, the Spirit of the Lord came upon David with strength, which he certainly needed up to and after the time he took the throne.

At some point in life, each of us will be called in a different direction. God transforms ex-convicts into preachers, draws businessmen into full-time missions, and impassions lay Christians to start ministries in their circles. Or He may adjust your family situation, your finances, or your health for His own purposes. These transitions can be difficult, to be sure—but when the Spirit of the Lord is directing you, you will find strength and courage to move forward.

THE MAN FOR THE HOUR

Joseph of Arimathea came, an honorable counselor,
who also waited for the kingdom of God, and went in
boldly to Pilate, and asked for the body of Jesus. And
Pilate marveled that He was already dead. And calling
the centurion, he asked him whether He was already
dead. And when he learned from the centurion, he gave
the body to Joseph. And he bought fine linen, and took
Him down, and wrapped Him in the linen, and laid
Him in a sepulchre that had been cut out of a rock,
and rolled a stone against the door of the sepulchre.

MARK 15:43–46 SKJV

God hath today somewhere, I know not where, in yon obscure cottage of an English village, or in a log-hut far away in the backwoods of America, or in the slums of our back streets, or in our palaces, a man who in maturer life shall deliver Israel, fighting the battles of the Lord. The Lord hath His servant making ready, and when the time shall come, when the hour shall want the man, the man shall be found for the hour. The Lord's will shall be done, let infidels and doubters think what they please. I see in this advent of Joseph of Arimathea exactly at the needed time, a well of consolation for all who have the cause of God laid upon their hearts. We need not worry our heads about who is to succeed the pastors and evangelists of today: the apostolical succession we may safely leave with our God.

DON'T WORRY

The righteous cry out, and the LORD hears them;
he delivers them from all their troubles. The LORD
is close to the brokenhearted and saves those who are
crushed in spirit. The righteous person may have many
troubles, but the LORD delivers him from them all.

PSALM 34:17–19 NIV

Worry. For some it's a constant companion on the road of life. Like the proverbial backseat driver, its mouth is constantly running, offering relentless, annoying, unnecessary warnings about every twist and turn, every bump and pothole, every possible direction on the road ahead.

What does God say about worry? Phrases like "do not be afraid" and "fear not" are said to occur 365 times in the Bible, one for every day of the year. So when it comes to worry, God simply says *don't*. For the believer it just isn't necessary.

In fact, worry is actually a kind of unfaithfulness. When we stress over our lives and the things we need, we're indicating that we don't really trust God. We're questioning whether He is big enough or concerned enough to know about those things and to work them all together for our good.

But worry doesn't have power to take away our problems. The only thing it takes away is our peace.

The psalm writer assures us that God hears when we cry out to Him. So today, remember to seek first His kingdom and righteousness. Don't worry about tomorrow. Let tomorrow worry about itself—*tomorrow*. Each day has enough trouble of its own.

PEACE!

I said to the one standing before me, "I am overcome
with anguish because of the vision, my lord, and I feel
very weak. How can I, your servant, talk with you, my
lord? My strength is gone and I can hardly breathe."
Again the one who looked like a man touched me and
gave me strength. "Do not be afraid, you who are highly
esteemed," he said. "Peace! Be strong now; be strong."
When he spoke to me, I was strengthened and said,
"Speak, my lord, since you have given me strength."
DANIEL 10:16–19 NIV

At this point in his story, Daniel could easily have been
ninety years old. What's more, he had been fasting for three
weeks. So when he saw a vision of a man with a body "like
topaz, his face like lightning, his eyes like flaming torches,
his arms and legs like the gleam of burnished bronze, and
his voice like the sound of a multitude" (verse 6), we can
forgive him for blanching (verse 8), fainting (verse 9),
trembling prostrate (verse 10), falling flat and speechless
(verse 15), experiencing anguish and powerlessness (verse
16), and feeling breathless (verse 17).

Deep fear produces four responses: to freeze, flee,
fight, or focus. They are not exclusive and certainly not
sequential. To reach the point of focus in fear, we first
need to find peace. So it's no wonder the Lord and His
angels frequently say things like, "Do not be afraid," "Be
strong," and "Peace!" whenever they appear.

For Christians, peace is a fruit of the Holy Spirit. The
more time we spend with God in His Word and prayer,
allowing His Spirit to work within us, the stronger we'll
be when fearful situations arise.

DOWNTURNS IN LIFE

Joseph's master took him and put him in prison,
the place where the king's prisoners were confined.
But while Joseph was there in the prison, the Lord
was with him; he showed him kindness and granted
him favor in the eyes of the prison warden.

Working for the Egyptian official Potiphar, Joseph always did the right thing. He respected Potiphar's business dealings. He respected Potiphar's possessions. He respected Potiphar's family. However, when Joseph rejected the advances of Potiphar's wife, she falsely accused him of assault—and Joseph found himself in prison.

Joseph could have responded to this downturn in his circumstances by complaining, crying, or casting off his trust in God. But his faith was not shaken. As he would later tell the brothers who had initially sold him into slavery, "God sent me ahead of you to preserve for you a remnant on earth and to save your lives by a great deliverance" (Genesis 45:7 NIV). We help ourselves by viewing present-day events from God's perspective, watching for His work even in our most difficult times.

Joseph quickly began to serve the prison warden, earning his trust as he had Potiphar's. Since God had faithfully met his needs in the past, Joseph knew God would provide in this situation also.

We will all face downturns in life, some minor and others overwhelming. When we do, remember that there is a God in heaven who desires our best. Keep your focus on Him and wait for His deliverance.

GOD IS FAITHFUL

David said to the Philistine, "You come against me
with sword and spear and javelin, but I come against
you in the name of the LORD Almighty, the God of
the armies of Israel, whom you have defied. This
day the LORD will deliver you into my hands."

1 SAMUEL 17:45–46 NIV

You've heard and read—countless times—the story of David slaying Goliath, the ten-foot-tall giant. You know that David accomplished that feat with a sling and five smooth stones. In fact, he killed the enemy with his first shot. But have you ever considered where David's confidence came from?

He didn't even wear armor in the battle. But that wasn't a chest-beating display of his own manliness. David just wanted to stand up for Israel and its soldiers (1 Samuel 17:26). He had confidence in the Lord, based on his previous experience.

As a shepherd, David had told King Saul, he had gone after lions and bears that attacked his flock, striking them and rescuing sheep from their mouths. At times, he even killed the predators. "This uncircumcised Philistine will be like one of them," David declared, "because he has defied the armies of the living God. The LORD who rescued me from the paw of the lion and the paw of the bear will rescue me from the hand of this Philistine" (1 Samuel 17:36–37).

When you are about to face your own Goliath, what story of God's faithfulness can you tell yourself? Take some time today to recall victories that He has given you—and you'll be armed with His confidence for the future.

ILL-EQUIPPED BUT READY

These were his instructions: "Take nothing for the journey except a staff—no bread, no bag, no money in your belts."

MARK 6:8 NIV

When Jesus sent His disciples out to witness to the Jews, He gave them the authority to drive out evil spirits and heal all kinds of sicknesses. But they probably felt ill-equipped for their mission.

How many times did Jesus teach the disciples, only to have them miss His point? They rarely understood His words the first time, and He often had to explain Himself.

Then, on the physical level, the Lord specifically prohibited the disciples from taking supplies for their journey. They could carry a walking stick, but that was it. For food, money, and other basic needs, they were to rely on God's provision alone.

Didn't Jesus understand what the disciples needed?

Of course He did, and His disciples went out and did what Jesus asked. If He had sent them out fully provisioned with bags of food and money, they wouldn't have depended on God's providence. If Jesus had waited to send the disciples until they felt fully knowledgeable, they would have relied on their own brains instead of allowing God to speak through them.

We will sometimes feel ill equipped for the task God has given us. But that's when we are perfectly positioned. We'll see that He can overcome our weakness with His strength.

ALL THE STRENGTH IN THE WORLD

*But God has chosen the foolish things of the world
to confound the wise, and God has chosen the weak
things of the world to confound the things that are
mighty. And God has chosen lowly things of the
world and things that are despised, yes, and things
that are not, to bring to nothing things that are,
that no person should boast in His presence.*

1 CORINTHIANS 1:27–29 SKJV

How it ought to encourage us all to believe we may each
have a part in building up the walls of the heavenly Zion.
In all ages God has delighted to use the weak things. In
his letter to the Corinthians Paul speaks of five things God
uses: foolish things, weak things, base things, despised
things, and things which are not. What for? "That no
flesh should glory in His presence."

When we are weak then we are strong. People often
think they have not strength enough; the fact is we have
too much strength. It is when we feel that we have no
strength of our own, that we are willing God should use us
and work through us. If we are leaning on God's strength,
we have more than all the strength of the world.

This world is not going to be reached by mere human
intellectual power. When we realize we have no strength,
then all the fulness of God will flow in upon us. Then we
shall have power with God and with man.

WHO'S YOUR BARNABAS?

*When [Saul] came to Jerusalem, he tried to join
the disciples, but they were all afraid of him, not
believing that he really was a disciple. But Barnabas
took him and brought him to the apostles.*

ACTS 9:26–27 NIV

Barnabas makes for an interesting study. His real name
was Joseph, and he came from the Mediterranean island
of Cyprus, about 250 miles from Jerusalem. Part of the
Jewish tribe of Levi, which produced Israel's priests, Joseph
first appears in Acts 4 shortly after the Holy Spirit's arrival
at Pentecost. Members of the early church were so unified
that they sold their possessions and gave generously to any
other Christians in need. Joseph sold a field and handed the
proceeds over to the apostles, who gave him the nickname
Barnabas: "son of encouragement."

The next time he appears in scripture, Barnabas is
encouraging an unlikely new believer named Saul—the
same Saul who had been rabidly persecuting Christians.
That changed when Jesus got Saul's attention on the
road to Damascus; the believers' understandable fear of
Saul changed when Barnabas stood up for him, bringing
the future apostle to the church leadership for a proper
introduction.

God has placed Barnabases in strategic locations to
encourage His people at just the right times. A Barnabas
may already have helped you; there may be one coming
into your life right now. Either way, be willing to accept
the encouragement he provides. And always look for ways
to be a Barnabas yourself.

STAND STRONG

*"Was that day the first time I [Ahimelek]
inquired of God for [David]? Of course not!
Let not the king [Saul] accuse your servant
or any of his father's family, for your servant
knows nothing at all about this whole affair."*

1 SAMUEL 22:15 NIV

Saul's jealousy against David was nearly consuming him.
The Spirit of God had left Saul (see 1 Samuel 16:14),
and he was being tormented by an evil spirit. These facts
help to explain why Saul reacted murderously when he
discovered that Ahimelek, a priest at Nob, had inquired
of the Lord for David, gave him provisions, and turned
over Goliath's sword.

When Saul questioned Ahimelek, the priest wondered why he wouldn't have helped David—the young
warrior was the king's most trusted servant (see 22:14).
But in a fit of raging jealousy, Saul had eighty-five priests
killed, in addition to women, children, and animals in
the town of Nob.

In Ahimelek's mind, he was simply serving his king by
inquiring of the Lord for the king's most trusted servant.
And he lost his life in the process. Sometimes doing the
right thing comes with a heavy cost. But God is always
faithful. He will give you the backbone required to stand
in the face of the harshest persecution. And if you end
up paying the ultimate sacrifice, the next face you see will
be that of Jesus.

GOD DELIGHTS TO ANSWER PRAYER

*And it shall come to pass, that before
they call, I will answer, and while
they are still speaking, I will hear.*
ISAIAH 65:24 SKJV

The scripture is full of such answers; every page of it encourages prayer. God will have us pray, and He will answer prayer.

Surely we have all found out that in our own experience; if not it is our own fault. "The arm of the Lord is not shortened, that it cannot save." It is our own prayers that are shortened and that are weak and faithless. Oh, let us "ask in faith, nothing wavering."

Some people are like the disciples in Jerusalem praying for the release of Peter; their prayers were answered, and Peter stood at the door, but they could not believe it; they said it must be his spirit. But, oh! Let us take God at His word. He says, "While they are yet speaking, I will hear." Is not that encouragement sufficient? He delights to hear our prayers; He will not weary with our often coming.

REMEMBER NOT TO FORGET

"My people are being destroyed because they don't know me. . . . Since you have forgotten the laws of your God, I will forget to bless your children."

HOSEA 4:6 NLT

Reading through the Old Testament, one marvels at the patience of God in dealing with His sinful people. But before we judge the ancient Israelites too harshly, consider that we as Christians—with God's Spirit living inside us—often fail Him too. And know that He has recorded the story of Israel as an example for us today (see 1 Corinthians 10:1–11).

Through the prophet Hosea, God told His people that they didn't even know Him. By their careless and selfish living, they had "forgotten the laws of [their] God," and in return, God would "forget" to bless their children. That's a heavy threat, coming from the loving, merciful, and powerful Creator of the universe.

It's certainly a warning to us today, but also a very simple guideline: Remember not to forget. Keep God and His laws in your thinking. Don't wander away from Him or them. Never override the prompting of His Spirit when He tells you to do (or not do) some particular thing.

If we remember not to forget God, we'll keep ourselves in His love, as Jude wrote (verse 21). Such a small effort on our part will pay large dividends of God's blessing—and courage for our daily challenges.

FIND COMFORT IN GOD

And Hannah prayed and said, My heart
rejoices in the LORD; my horn is exalted in the
LORD. My mouth is enlarged over my enemies,
because I rejoice in Your salvation.

1 SAMUEL 2:1 SKJV

It is very beautiful to see how the saints of old time were accustomed to find comfort in their God. When they came into sore straits, when troubles multiplied, when helpers failed, when earthly comforts were removed, they were accustomed to look to the Lord and to the Lord alone. Thus Hannah thinks of the Lord and comforts herself in His name. By this means they were made strong and glad: they began to sing instead of sighing, and to work wonders instead of fainting under their burdens, even as here the inspired poetess sings, "My heart rejoiceth in the LORD, mine horn is exalted in the LORD." To them God was a reality, a present reality, and they looked to Him as their rock of refuge, their helper and defense, a very present help in time of trouble.

Can we not at the outset learn a valuable lesson from their example? Let us do as they did; let us lean upon our God and stay ourselves upon Him when heart and flesh are failing.

GOD DOES IT

*Pharaoh said to Joseph, "I had a dream, and no
one can interpret it. But I have heard it said of you
that when you hear a dream you can interpret it."
"I cannot do it," Joseph replied to Pharaoh, "but
God will give Pharaoh the answer he desires."*

GENESIS 41:15–16 NIV

It was an intense dream, and Pharaoh knew it contained
significant information. He simply did not know the
interpretation of the dream. The Egyptian ruler sought
the advice of his best counselors, the finest minds in all
the land, but they didn't understand the dream either.
Thankfully, one of Pharaoh's employees knew an individual
who could help.

Sometime before, Pharaoh's butler had offended his
boss and spent time in prison. There he met Joseph, a
Hebrew slave from the house of Potiphar. The butler had
also experienced a troubling dream, and young Joseph had
provided an interpretation that proved to be 100 percent
accurate. In this moment of Pharaoh's need, the butler
remembered Joseph.

Summoned to the palace, Joseph was indeed able to
provide the interpretation of Pharaoh's dream. It was a
moment in which Joseph could boast, saying, "Look at
me!" Instead, he declared the glory of God. Joseph refused
to take credit because he understood a simple fact: God
provides His children with wisdom, strength, and courage
for their time of need.

We too can count on those blessings. We too should
give God the glory.

FEAR GOD, NOT MAN

Once again David inquired of the LORD, and the
LORD answered him, "Go down to Keilah, for I
am going to give the Philistines into your hand."

1 SAMUEL 23:4 NIV

After learning that enemy soldiers were looting the threshing floor in Keilah—a city in southern Judah near the
border with the Philistines—David had one question
for the Lord: "Shall I go and attack these Philistines?"
(1 Samuel 23:2 NIV).

Even though the Lord said yes, David's men weren't
ready for battle. They admitted that they were afraid even
living in Judah. Perhaps they feared retaliation from King
Saul for aligning themselves with David. Maybe they even
wondered if some among their number were loyal to Saul.
So David inquired of the Lord again and was given the
same answer. He and his men went to battle and inflicted
heavy losses on the Philistines.

We as Christians are like David's men. We will certainly face opposition for standing with Jesus, from friends
or coworkers and maybe even our families. When the Lord
sent out His twelve disciples, He promised them opposition (see Matthew 10:23; Luke 21:12; John 15:20). But
here's what He told them: "Do not be afraid of those who
kill the body but cannot kill the soul. Rather, be afraid
of the One who can destroy both soul and body in hell"
(Matthew 10:28 NIV).

In other words, have more reverence for God than
fear of man. God is stronger, wiser, and more loving than
we can even imagine. He'll take care of us.

CLOTHED WITH CHRIST

*But the Spirit of the LORD came
on Gideon, and he blew a trumpet.
And the Abiezrites gathered around him.*
JUDGES 6:34 SKJV

We read in Judges, "The Spirit of the LORD came upon Gideon." But you know that there is in the New Testament an equally wonderful text, where we read, "Put ye on the Lord Jesus Christ" (Romans 13:14), that is, clothe yourself with Christ Jesus.

And what does that mean? It does not only mean, by imputation of righteousness outside of me, but to clothe myself with the living character of the living Christ, with the living love of the living Christ. Put on the Lord Jesus. Oh! What a work.

I cannot do it unless I believe and understand that He whom I have to put on is as a garment covering my whole being. I have to put on a living Christ who has said, "Lo, I am with you always" (Matthew 28:20). Just draw the folds closer round you of that robe of light with which Christ would array you. Just come and acknowledge that Christ is with you, on you, in you. Oh, put Him on!

SURPRISING HELP

*Once safely on shore, we found out that the
island was called Malta. The islanders showed us
unusual kindness. They built a fire and welcomed
us all because it was raining and cold.*

ACTS 28:1–2 NIV

Saul, the man who would become the apostle Paul, was converted by the direct intervention of Jesus Himself. Throughout his career as a missionary, church leader, and Bible author, Paul enjoyed fellowship with other believers, interactions with angels, and even conversations with God through heavenly visions. God had promised that Paul would suffer for His name (see Acts 9:16), but the Lord also provided strong supports for His servant.

In the last chapter of Acts, we see Paul getting support from a surprising source—the pagan inhabitants of the island of Malta. Though these people didn't know the one true God (they thought Paul himself was a god when a snakebite didn't kill him), they were compassionate to the great missionary and his traveling companions, whose ship had broken apart in a storm.

That's just like God, who can use any person or nation or situation to accomplish His will. Think of the Persian king, Cyrus, restoring the Jewish nation. Or Jonah's fish. Or even the horrible choices of Judas Iscariot that led to Jesus' death on the cross. . .and the salvation of everyone who believes.

When life is hard, as is often the case, be ready for God to help—from the expected sources or even from the surprising ones.

SINS CAST AWAY

Behold, for peace I had great bitterness,
but in love for my soul You have delivered
it from the pit of corruption, for You have
cast all my sins behind Your back.

ISAIAH 38:17 SKJV

The terrible name of sin! How it used to haunt me in my early years! I thought all my sins would be blazed out before the Great White Throne; that every sin committed in childhood and in secret, and every secret thought, and every evil desire, would be just blazed out before the assembled universe; that everything done in the dark would be brought to light.

But thanks be to God, the gospel tells me my sins are all put away in Christ. Out of love to my soul, He has taken all my sins and cast them behind His back. That is a safe place to have our sins cast away—behind God's back. God never turns back; He always marches on. He will never see your sins if they are behind His back.

That is one of His own illustrations. Out of love to my soul, He has taken all my sins upon Him. Not a part. He takes them all out of the way. "The blood of Jesus Christ His Son cleanseth us from all sin" (1 John 1:7).

HE WILL STRENGTHEN YOU

But the Lord is faithful;
he will strengthen you and
guard you from the evil one.
2 Thessalonians 3:3 nlt

Could there be a clearer promise than this verse?

The apostle Paul, who wrote 2 Thessalonians, also penned the letter to the Ephesians. In it, he said, "We are not fighting against flesh-and-blood enemies, but against evil rulers and authorities of the unseen world, against mighty powers in this dark world, and against evil spirits in the heavenly places" (6:12 nlt). Paul wasn't trying to scare people—he just wanted Christians to be realistic. We are not capable of winning our battles on our own.

But that's where God comes in. He is faithful, Paul said, to "strengthen" us. In the context of 2 Thessalonians 3, Paul was discussing God's help in sharing the gospel, His protection from wicked people (verse 2), and His enabling to follow biblical commands (verse 4). If we allow Him, God will lead us "into a full understanding and expression of the love of God and the patient endurance that comes from Christ" (verse 5 nlt).

The key question is, will we allow God to do His work in our lives? Will we submit to His authority, study His Word, pray for His blessing, and serve His people? Every time we say yes, He provides the strength we need to move forward.

OUR SUREST ROAD TO HAPPINESS

The generous soul shall be made prosperous,
and he who waters shall also be watered himself.
PROVERBS 11:25 SKJV

The general principle is, that in living for the good of others, we shall be profited also ourselves. We must not isolate our own interests but feel that we live for others.

This teaching is sustained by the analogy of nature, for in nature there is a law that no one thing can be independent of the rest of creation, but there is a mutual action and reaction of all upon all. All the constituent parts of the universe are bound to one another by invisible chains, and there is not a single creature in it which springeth up, or flourisheth, or decayeth for itself alone. The very planets, though they float far from one another, exercise attraction; and the fixed stars, though they seem to be infinitely remote, are still linked to one another by mysterious bonds.

God has so constituted this universe that selfishness is the greatest possible offense against His law, and living for others, and ministering to others, is the strictest obedience to His will. Our surest road to our own happiness is to seek the good of our fellows.

OVERCOME EVIL WITH GOOD

[David] said to his men, "The LORD forbid that I should
do such a thing to my master, the LORD's anointed,
or lay my hand on him; for he is the anointed of the
LORD." With these words David sharply rebuked
his men and did not allow them to attack Saul.

1 SAMUEL 24:6–7 NIV

This was David's perfect opportunity to take out his powerful persecutor. As King Saul was pursuing David, he ducked into a cave to use the restroom. It was a cave David himself was hiding in.

David's men encouraged him to kill Saul, assuming that the Lord had arranged this opportunity. But David knew better and resisted the urge to sin.

"He not only would not do this bad thing himself, but he would not suffer those about him to do it," the old-time commentator Matthew Henry wrote. "Thus he rendered good for evil, to him from whom he received evil for good; and was herein an example to all who are called Christians, not to be overcome of evil, but to overcome evil with good."

The apostle Paul picks up this theme in Romans 12:21 (NIV): "Do not be overcome by evil, but overcome evil with good."

As Christians, we all have opportunities to sin against our enemies. But with God's Holy Spirit living inside us, we dare not give in to our baser instincts. If we submit to the Spirit, He'll provide all the strength we need to overcome evil with good.

CLEAN HANDS, CLEAN HEART

*"Nothing outside a person can defile them
by going into them. Rather, it is what comes
out of a person that defiles them."*

MARK 7:15 NIV

Washing hands is important. To keep our bodies safe from germs, it's wise to wash our hands frequently for a minimum of twenty seconds. But no amount of handwashing can clean us from the spiritual sickness within.

When the Pharisees caught Jesus' disciples eating food with unwashed hands, they asked the Lord why His disciples didn't follow the Jewish handwashing rituals. Jesus fired back, asking why the Pharisees followed the traditions of the elders instead of the Word of God.

To Jesus, having unwashed hands was a physical issue, not a spiritual one. The Pharisees were so concerned about their outward ritual cleanliness that they ignored the spiritual filth corrupting their hearts.

To be physically healthy, washing our hands is a good idea. To be spiritually healthy, we must ask the Lord to cleanse us from the inside out. As Jesus said, "It is from within, out of a person's heart, that evil thoughts come—sexual immorality, theft, murder, adultery, greed, malice, deceit, lewdness, envy, slander, arrogance and folly" (Mark 7:21–22 NIV).

And Jesus is ready and able to do the job. According to 1 John 1:9, "If we confess our sins, he is faithful and just and will forgive us our sins and purify us from all unrighteousness" (NIV).

GOD IS ALWAYS TRUE

*"And afterward, I will pour out my Spirit on
all people. Your sons and daughters will prophesy,
your old men will dream dreams, your young men
will see visions. Even on my servants, both men and
women, I will pour out my Spirit in those days."*

Joel 2:28–29 niv

Joel's prophecies address events in his day, events during
the founding of the early church, and still other events at
the climax of history.

Today's verses figure prominently on the church's
birthday, the day of Pentecost, shortly after Jesus Christ's
ascension to God the Father's right hand.

As promised (Acts 1:4–5), Jesus sent the Holy Spirit
(2:4) upon His 120 followers (1:15, 2:1). The Spirit's
arrival was accompanied by the sound of a mighty rushing
wind (2:2). His filling of the first Christians was marked
by small flames of fire above each (2:3) and their speaking
in foreign languages they didn't previously know (2:4).

All this commotion attracted a lot of attention. Jews
from around the known world had gathered in Jerusalem
for Pentecost. An international crowd of thousands formed
(2:5–6, 41). They marveled to hear Christ followers speaking in their mother tongues (2:7–11). They wondered
what was happening.

Then Peter stood up, filled with the Spirit, and
preached the life-changing gospel of Jesus Christ. He
quickly explained that they were all witnessing the fulfillment of Joel's prophecy quoted above (2:16–18).

It's true, three thousand people affirmed. And they
were baptized that day (Acts 2:41).

MUTUAL ENCOURAGEMENT

*I long to see you so that I may impart to you some
spiritual gift to make you strong—that is, that you and
I may be mutually encouraged by each other's faith.*

ROMANS 1:11–12 NIV

The apostle Paul mentions spiritual gifts in Romans 1,
then explains them in greater detail in chapter 12. These
gifts hold immense value to the Christian community.
The abilities bestowed by God's Spirit—things like serving, teaching, encouraging, and giving—vary from person to person. But when they are shared within the church,
they create mutual benefit, blessing both the giver and
the receiver.

"Iron sharpens iron," the Proverbs say, "so one person
sharpens another" (27:17 NIV). There is great strength to
be found in the church—the worldwide "body of Christ"
that is made up of the local congregations all around us.
That's one reason the writer of Hebrews tells Christian
believers, "Let us not neglect our meeting together, as some
people do, but encourage one another, especially now that
the day of [Jesus'] return is drawing near" (10:25 NLT).

Paul wanted to share his gifts with the church at
Rome. He knew that that would help the believers there,
but also encourage him. The principle still stands today.
Find courage for your challenges by being involved in a
local, Bible-believing church.

LOOK FROM MAN TO GOD

This is what the LORD says: "Cursed is the man
who trusts in man and makes flesh his arm,
and whose heart departs from the LORD."
JEREMIAH 17:5 SKJV

If there is going to be a great work done here, God must do the work. It is not any new gospel that is wanted; it is not any new power. It is the same old power—the power of the Holy Ghost; and it is the same old story—the story of redeeming love—nothing new.

The world is running here and there after something new, and they come and hear the old, old story, and they say, "Well, it is not anything new after all." If you have come here expecting to hear something new, you will be disappointed. We are just going to preach the same old truths your ministers before have been preaching. And not only that, but we are come in weakness; and if you are leaning upon man you will be disappointed. "Cursed is the man that maketh the arm of flesh his trust."

But if we lean upon God and all our expectations are from Him, we shall not be disappointed. What we want is to cease from man and get done with man and look right away straight from man up to God.

INVITATION TO RETURN

"In those days and in that time," says the LORD,
"the children of Israel shall come, they and the children
of Judah together; going and weeping they shall go,
and seek the LORD their God. They shall ask the
way to Zion, with their faces toward there, saying,
'Come and let us join ourselves to the LORD in a
perpetual covenant that shall not be forgotten.'"

JEREMIAH 50:4–5 SKJV

We, too, by nature are in banishment, far off from our God and the abode of His glory. We are not what we ought to have been, for the Lord did not make us to be sinners, but to be His happy and obedient creatures: our present lost estate is not our true state; we are banished through coming under the power of our great adversary; sin has carried us into captivity; we are in the far country, away from the great Father's house.

It is a great blessing when the times come, and they have come, when there is an opportunity and an invitation to return. Today the power of the adversary is broken, and we may flee out of the Babylon of sin. A greater than Cyrus has opened the two-leaved gates and broken the bars of iron in sunder and proclaimed liberty to the captives. We may now return to our God and freely enjoy the holy and happy associations, which belong to the City of our God.

THE GATEWAY TO SAVING FAITH

*"And everyone who calls on the
name of the LORD will be saved."*
JOEL 2:32 NIV

The day the church began, three thousand heard Peter's
gospel sermon, believed and were saved, and were then
baptized (Acts 2:41). How good that the Lord loves to
save people instantly, forever!

But scripture also makes it clear that some people
take longer. Just witness Peter himself. The impetuous,
think-aloud disciple followed Jesus for three years and
still didn't understand much of the faith life. Only after
Jesus' resurrection, appearances, ascension, and sending
of the Holy Spirit did Peter become the world-changing
apostle we recognize.

So, is someone "who calls on the name of the LORD"
saved instantly or eventually? Yes. Some have little knowledge of the Lord, but they're desperate (Joel 1:13–15,
2:15–17). Others have some knowledge and are ready to
cross the line. Still others call on the Lord several times
before they become real Christians.

Nobody races from 0 to 60 in their knowledge of
God. In this life, we do well to keep walking in the right
direction in obedience to our Lord and Savior.

Still, Peter gladly quoted today's key verse in his first
evangelistic sermon (Acts 2:21) and the apostle Paul also
did so in one of his most important letters (Romans 10:13).

Whatever struggles you may face in life, there is one
answer: call on the name of the Lord. He will be faithful
to save you.

GOD HAS A PLAN

Then Joseph said to his brothers, "Come close to me." When they had done so, he said, "I am your brother Joseph, the one you sold into Egypt! And now, do not be distressed and do not be angry with yourselves for selling me here, because it was to save lives that God sent me ahead of you. For two years now there has been famine in the land, and for the next five years there will be no plowing and reaping. But God sent me ahead of you to preserve for you a remnant on earth and to save your lives by a great deliverance."

GENESIS 45:4–7 NIV

Even though they had hated him, betrayed him, and told their father he was dead, Joseph was very gracious to his brothers. At this reunion, he comforted them by acknowledging God's providence. This is certainly commendable, but Joseph had the blessing of hindsight. The difficulties of his challenge were past.

Where do we find courage when we're still in the middle of trouble? When times get tough we may wonder if God has a plan. How do we find strength to keep following Him when the future is bleak?

Allow God to work. His solutions to life's problems are often the result of lengthy seasons of prayer. It may take time (and certainly our willingness) for Him to adjust the hearts and minds of all involved.

Joseph was likely a teenager when he was sold into slavery. He was probably approaching forty when he reconciled with his family. God's timing may seem slow to us, but He understands the past and knows the future: "The plans of the LORD stand firm forever, the purposes of his heart through all generations" (Psalm 33:11 NIV).

TABLE SCRAPS

The woman was a Greek, born in Syrian Phoenicia.
She begged Jesus to drive the demon out of her daughter.
"First let the children eat all they want," he told her, "for
it is not right to take the children's bread and toss it to the
dogs." "Lord," she replied, "even the dogs under the table
eat the children's crumbs." Then he told her, "For such a
reply, you may go; the demon has left your daughter."
MARK 7:26–29 NIV

Jesus Christ is the Savior of the world. But when He started His ministry, He went first to the children of Israel. Jesus showed the Jews signs that He was the Messiah they had been waiting for. But they rejected Jesus and handed Him over to the Romans for execution. Israel's loss became the whole world's gain.

That is the background of today's passage. Even so, it might be surprising to see Jesus respond to a Gentile woman's request by essentially calling her a dog. Perhaps it was because "dog" was a common Jewish name for Gentiles. Maybe Jesus was playing on a stereotype of Jews to test whether the woman's faith was genuine. Whatever the reason, her response to Jesus' rebuff showed faithful persistence. If His slur was a test, the Syrophoenician woman passed.

When we pray—whether we're asking God for a healing or anything else—we must show the same faithful persistence. We can't let the fear of rejection keep us from making requests to the only one strong enough to help. Since the gospel has been opened up to the whole world, we can confidently go to the Father any time. We don't have to beg for table scraps!

GLORY IN SUFFERINGS?

Not only so, but we also glory in our sufferings, because we know that suffering produces perseverance; perseverance, character; and character, hope. And hope does not put us to shame, because God's love has been poured out into our hearts through the Holy Spirit, who has been given to us.

ROMANS 5:3–5 NIV

It might be hard to imagine joy in suffering. But this is what the apostle Paul discovered.

He knew all about difficulties and opposition. In becoming a follower of Jesus, Paul betrayed the Jewish sect he'd been born into. And as he became an outspoken Christian leader, Paul put himself directly in the path of the persecution he had previously dealt out.

But following Jesus' footsteps, no matter the opposition, became Paul's mission. He knew that trouble would come but also that he was serving the living God. Paul viewed persecution as an opportunity for growth, a chance to experience the love of Christ.

As with so many aspects of the Christian life, this mindset runs counter to our human expectations. Glory in suffering? Yes, it is possible. And, even more than possible, it is a promise to faithful believers. As Paul wrote, "We also glory in our sufferings, because we know that suffering produces perseverance; perseverance, character; and character, hope. And hope does not put us to shame, because God's love has been poured out into our hearts through the Holy Spirit, who has been given to us."

Hard times are certain. But so is God's ability to use them for your good.

REMEMBER HIS FAITHFULNESS

*But David thought to himself, "One of these days I
will be destroyed by the hand of Saul. The best thing
I can do is to escape to the land of the Philistines.
Then Saul will give up searching for me anywhere
in Israel, and I will slip out of his hand."*

1 SAMUEL 27:1 NIV

When we've been in a long spiritual battle, we're prone to
become weary—maybe even doubtful of God's provision
and protection. That seems to be the case with David in
today's passage. On the run from the jealous king, David
had enjoyed God's protection time and time again. In 1
Samuel 26, we even see Saul withdrawing from David,
parting with a blessing (verse 25).

David was understandably skeptical of Saul. But
he shouldn't have been so with God. Weariness, fear,
and doubt caused David to do the unthinkable: seek
refuge among the Philistines, the implacable enemies of
God's people.

This world abounds with hardships—some of our own
creation and others that are imposed upon us. Whatever
the case, Satan is happy to use our trials to keep us from
God. Like David, though, we know that God has often
brought us through difficulties in the past. Remembering
His faithfulness will give us courage to overcome whatever
trials we're currently facing.

GOD IS MOVED BY MISERY

And she called the name of the LORD who
spoke to her "You, God, See Me," for she said,
"Have I also here looked after Him who sees me?"
GENESIS 16:13 SKJV

Although there was no prayer of Hagar's for God to hear, another voice spake in His ear. The angel who suddenly appeared to her said, "The Lord hath heard thy affliction." That is a very beautiful sentence. Thou hast not prayed: thou hast been willful, reckless, and at last despairing, and therefore thou hast not cried unto the Lord. But thy deep sorrow has cried to Him.

Thou art oppressed, and the Lord has undertaken for thee. Thou art suffering heavily, and God, the All-pitiful, has heard thy affliction. Grief has an eloquent voice when mercy is the listener. Woe has a plea which goodness cannot resist. Though sorrow and woe ought to be attended with prayer, yet even when supplication is not offered, the heart of God is moved by misery itself.

In Hagar's case, the Lord heard her affliction: He looked forth from His glory upon that lone Egyptian woman who was in the deepest distress in which a woman could well be placed, and He came speedily to her help.

WALK BY FAITH

So Achish called David and said to him, "As surely as the LORD lives, you have been reliable, and I would be pleased to have you serve with me in the army. From the day you came to me until today, I have found no fault in you, but the rulers don't approve of you."

1 SAMUEL 29:6 NIV

David found himself in a real dilemma when the Philistine king, Achish, called him to fight against Israel. David and his men, on the run from King Saul, had found refuge with the enemy Philistines. Now it was time to show David's true allegiance.

Bible commentator Adam Clarke points out that if David had gone into battle, he would have had his choice between two sins: fight for the Philistines (thereby opposing God's chosen people) or deceive and oppose Achish (who had treated David hospitably).

Other Philistine leaders, knowing that David was a celebrated warrior of Israel, objected. So Achish ultimately sent David away from the battlefield.

"God, therefore, so ordered it in His mercy that he was not permitted to go to a battle in which he was sure to be disgraced, whatever side he took, or with what success so ever he might be crowned," Clarke wrote.

David was in a pickle of his own making, but God still delivered him.

The lesson isn't to behave recklessly and wait for God to sort things out. But know that, even when we sin, He is gracious and ready to forgive. Whatever dilemmas you may face, trust God to show you the way as you walk by faith.

A FRIGHTENING EXPERIENCE

A young man, wearing nothing but a linen garment, was following Jesus. When they seized him, he fled naked, leaving his garment behind.

MARK 14:51–52 NIV

The place: Gethsemane. The situation: Jesus is being arrested. Mark records a character unmentioned by the other Gospel writers: a naked man.

Imagine the setting: Judas has given his infamous kiss. Soldiers stand with representatives of the high priest. Peter whips out a sword and cuts off someone's ear. Jesus is seized, taken away for judgment and execution.

The moment of Jesus' arrest must have filled His disciples with terror. The center of their universe, the strongest man among them, had just showed weakness. He could have said a word to stop the whole thing, but He didn't. Now He was being led away by soldiers.

When a young follower of Christ followed a little too closely, soldiers seized him too. He only got away by shrugging out of his clothes, more willing to face the shame of public nudity than to share Jesus' fate. After all, if Jesus was too weak for the soldiers, what chance did any of the disciples have?

But Jesus wasn't being weak. He was applying His awesome strength to one of hardest things for anyone: self-sacrifice. The naked man in the garden sacrificed his clothes to save his life. Jesus would sacrifice His life to save the world from sin.

We who follow Jesus today have the strength of the Holy Spirit in our lives. He will help us through every frightening experience.

DISPENSE WITH PRIDE

*"The pride of your heart has deceived you, you who
live in the clefts of the rocks and make your home
on the heights, you who say to yourself, 'Who can
bring me down to the ground?' Though you soar like
the eagle and make your nest among the stars, from
there I will bring you down," declares the LORD.*

OBADIAH 3–4 NIV

The shortest prophetic book, Obadiah, warns of the Lord's
judgment on Edom. The Edomites were descendants of
Esau, twin brother of Jacob—father of the twelve tribes of
Israel. Despite the close family connection, the Edomites
despised God and rejected His chosen people.

Sometime after the fall of Jerusalem, Obadiah received
a brief but stirring message from the Lord that Edom was
next in line for destruction (1–14, 18).

The sins of Edom included acting arrogantly, deserting the southern kingdom of Judah, plundering Judah's
wealth, killing those who tried to escape, and handing
over survivors to the dreaded Babylonians.

Obadiah's brevity wasn't all the Lord had to say about
Edom's judgment. Jeremiah, Ezekiel, and Amos all prophesied trouble as well, and the recurring theme was Edom's
confidence in its own invincibility. Humanly speaking,
there is no such thing.

That's why we as Christians are wise to dispense with
pride. "God opposes the proud but shows favor to the
humble" (James 4:6; 1 Peter 5:5 NIV). No foundation is
weaker than our own perceived strength. None is greater
than God's favor. The choice is yours.

UNAFRAID

Who shall separate us from the love of Christ?
Shall trouble or hardship or persecution or famine
or nakedness or danger or sword? As it is written:
"For your sake we face death all day long;
we are considered as sheep to be slaughtered."
No, in all these things we are more than
conquerors through him who loved us.

ROMANS 8:35–37 NIV

Most of us have shelter. In the west, at least, famine is not one of our great fears. Nor are we generally afraid of being attacked in the places we frequent. In the times of the early church, however, these were legitimate fears. Persecution sometimes chased believers from their homes. Drought could affect crops and finances and even one's ability to eat. And a trip down a remote lane could result in danger from robbers lying in wait.

Today, our hardships typically take different forms. But fear—of our future and our fate—often remains, just as it did for the people of Paul's day.

That's why the apostle wanted believers to know, with absolute certainty, that the love of Christ can obliterate all fear. Through our Lord Jesus, we are free to live without fear and able to weather any challenge life throws at us.

Life comes with great uncertainty. But take comfort in the fact that nothing we experience can ever remove the deep and strengthening love of Jesus.

STRENGTH FROM GOD

David was greatly distressed because the men were talking of stoning him; each one was bitter in spirit because of his sons and daughters. But David found strength in the LORD his God.

1 SAMUEL 30:6 NIV

Israel's future king, David, had a strange sojourn in Philistine territory. As King Saul sought the younger man's life, David and his band of men hid out among Israel's enemies. David even developed a friendly relationship with the Philistine leader Achish.

Achish wanted David to accompany his army in battle against Israel, but other Philistine leaders demanded he return to Ziklag, a Philistine town Achish had given David. Before he and his men arrived, though, the Amalekites—a nomadic tribe who were also enemies of Israel—invaded. They carried away all the wives and children of David's band, including his wives, Ahinoam and Abigail. Then the Amalekites burned the city.

David's men were furious with him for exposing their families to such an attack. But as they talked about stoning him, today's verse says David found strength from the Lord. What did that look like, practically speaking?

For David, it meant prayer. He went straight to God to ask what his next steps should be. God answered with good news: David would recover all the kidnapped women and children.

In times of stress and upheaval, we can (and should) turn to God. "It is God who works in you," Philippians 2:13 (NIV) says, "to will and to act in order to fulfill his good purpose."

CRY TO GOD

*For the people shall dwell in Zion at Jerusalem.
You shall weep no longer. He will be very
gracious to you at the sound of your cry.
When He hears it, He will answer you.*

ISAIAH 30:19 SKJV

I desire at this time to set forth the graciousness of God and His readiness to listen to the cry of the needy, with the hope that some here present who may have forgotten this, to whom it may be a time of need, may hear it and be encouraged to say, "I will arise and go to my Father."

It is joy to me to hope that it will be so, but I remember with sadness that if I should be helped to set this forth clearly, and if any of you who are in trouble should afterwards refuse to trust in the Lord, your alienation will be aggravated, your sin will become still more crying.

He who will not trust when he knows that the Lord will be gracious to him sins against his own soul and plunges himself in sevenfold wrath. If the Lord saith that he will be very gracious at the voice of your cry, what must be your doom if you will not cry?

FEAR THE LORD

[Jonah] said to them, "I am a Hebrew, and I fear the LORD, the God of heaven, who has made the sea and the dry land." Then the men were exceedingly afraid, and said to him, "Why have you done this?" For the men knew that he fled from the presence of the LORD because he had told them.

JONAH 1:9–10 SKJV

It's possible to say good things about God without really meaning them. Such is the case with Jonah's statement to the pagan sailors manning the ship he was on.

Jonah told the truth about his nationality, but he lied about fearing the Lord God, Creator of heaven and earth and seas. At that moment, Jonah was arrogantly, defiantly, disobeying God by taking a ship in the opposite direction from the place he was called to.

Still, Jonah's acknowledgment of a "fear of the Lord" offers useful insights to our strength and success today. Recognizing God's awesome power, knowledge, and holiness should cause a certain amount of fear in us—the kind a mouse undoubtedly feels in the presence of a human being. But biblical fear is also a reverent respect, a desire to know and honor and, ultimately, enjoy an eternal relationship with this awesome God, who is also love—demonstrated by the sacrificial death of His Son, Jesus Christ (Romans 5:8).

As sinful human beings, we're pulled in many directions by our own emotions, temptations, companions, and culture. But when we truly acknowledge and "fear" the Lord, He will happily guide and strengthen us in His will.

THE PATH TO VICTORY

Moses answered the people, "Do not be afraid.
Stand firm and you will see the deliverance the
LORD will bring you today. The Egyptians you
see today you will never see again. The LORD
will fight for you; you need only to be still."

EXODUS 14:13–14 NIV

The nation of Israel was finally leaving its captivity in Egypt. But now the people found themselves pursued by the Egyptian army. In front of them lay the Red Sea, a seemingly impenetrable obstacle. Their dream of freedom appeared to be ending badly.

What the people forgot was that the Lord of heaven, the God of Abraham, was more powerful than the armies of Egypt. They had yet to understand that their God, the God of Moses, was able to overcome the obstacle of the Red Sea. In just a few short hours, the people would walk across dry ground after God performed a spectacular miracle. And soon after that, the army of Egypt would be annihilated in another spectacular miracle.

The Lord was ready to fight for Israel, just as He is ready to fight for believers in Christ today. The apostle John gives us this specific encouragement: "Everyone born of God overcomes the world. This is the victory that has overcome the world, even our faith" (1 John 5:4 NIV).

This promise is our path to victory. Faith will cause us to overcome, regardless of the obstacles we face.

STILL NEED TO FIGHT

*That was the beginning of a long war between those
who were loyal to Saul and those loyal to David. As
time passed David became stronger and stronger,
while Saul's dynasty became weaker and weaker.*

2 SAMUEL 3:1 NLT

Saul and his son Jonathan—David's beloved friend—were
killed by the Philistines. Saul's death led to David being
anointed king of Judah. But Saul's men in the northern sections of Israel were faithful to him, going so far as to anoint
Ishbosheth, another son of Saul, as king. War ensued.

David was God's chosen king for Israel, but he still
had to fight for his realm.

We as Christians are given a kingdom too (see Luke
12:32). But there will be a fight—in fact plenty of battles—before we find peace and comfort. We'll face many
hardships, but the apostle Paul assured us that they will be
worth it: "Since we are [God's] children, we are his heirs.
In fact, together with Christ we are heirs of God's glory.
But if we are to share his glory, we must also share his
suffering. Yet what we suffer now is nothing compared to
the glory he will reveal to us later" (Romans 8:17–18 NLT).

If God calls us to "share" in Jesus' suffering, He will
provide the power to do so. And He promises rewards we
can hardly imagine. You still need to fight, so step up to
the battle lines.

COURAGE FOR ANXIETY

For God has not given us a spirit of fear and
timidity, but of power, love, and self-discipline.
2 Timothy 1:7 nlt

Does it help you to realize that some key Bible characters dealt with anxiety and fear?

Notice how the apostle Paul speaks to Timothy in today's verse. This follows Paul describing Timothy as "my dear son" (1:2), a phrase he would repeat in 2:1, and noting Timothy's tears when he and the apostle had last parted (1:4). We get the impression that Timothy was a gentle and loving man, which is a positive thing. But because of his tenderness, Timothy might have struggled with the demands of leading the church in Ephesus.

So Paul encouraged the younger man with the words of 2 Timothy 1:7. When we are feeling the effects of anxiety on our lives, this verse is a wonderful reminder of God's provision. Fear, anxiety, and depression are not things that the Lord gives us. He may allow us to experience them for our growth, but if He does, there's a good reason.

In those moments, return to this scripture. Know for sure that God has given you a spirit of power, of love, and of self-discipline. Use this reminder to give yourself courage.

GOD IS PACIFIED

*"And I will establish My covenant with you. And you
shall know that I am the* LORD*, that you may remember
and be confounded, and never open your mouth anymore
because of your shame, when I am pacified toward
you for all that you have done," says the Lord* GOD.

EZEKIEL 16:62–63 SKJV

O believer, God is pacified towards you, for your sin is
covered; it is put away, all of it, and altogether. Since you
have believed in Jesus Christ your sin has not become
dimly visible, neither by searching may it be seen as a
shadow in the distance; but God seeth it no more forever.

And you may say, "O God, I will praise thee, for
though thou wast angry with me, thine anger is turned
away, and thou comfortedest me " (Isaiah 12:1). The many,
the countless hosts of sin that you have committed since
your childhood are all scattered as a cloud, and the one
black sin, which cost you more regret than many scores
of others, has been removed as a thick cloud. They are all
gone—no enemy remaineth. They cannot rise against you
from the grave; no, not one of them, while sun and moon
endure, nay, while God endureth, for, He saith, "They
shall not be mentioned against thee anymore, forever."

God is pacified towards His people for all that
they have done, altogether pacified, for their sins have
ceased to be.

YOU CAN'T OUT-SIN GRACE

For I am convinced that neither death nor life,
neither angels nor demons, neither the present nor the
future, nor any powers, neither height nor depth, nor
anything else in all creation, will be able to separate us
from the love of God that is in Christ Jesus our Lord.

ROMANS 8:38–39 NIV

Jesus often visited people's homes to eat dinner and teach on the kingdom of God. One such visit, at the home of Simon the Pharisee, is recorded in Luke 7. During the meal, a "sinful woman" poured perfume on His feet, wept over them, and wiped them dry with her hair.

As Simon grumbled to himself, Jesus told him a parable: "Two people owed money to a certain money-lender. One owed him five hundred denarii, and the other fifty. Neither of them had the money to pay him back, so he forgave the debts of both. Now which of them will love him more?" (Luke 7:41–42 NIV). Simon suggested the one with the larger debt. Jesus agreed.

Then Jesus turned to the woman. Instead of saying thank you, He told her that her sins were forgiven. The audience was stunned, and her life was changed.

At times, we all need forgiveness. Perhaps we've drifted away from God, or some overwhelming life experience breaks our fellowship with Him. But no matter where we've been or how much we've sinned, we can't out-sin God's grace through Jesus Christ. As the apostle Paul put it in Romans 8, nothing can pry us away from God's love. Like the prodigal son, you can always return to His home.

OUR TRUSTWORTHY GOD

*"I have been with you wherever you have gone,
and I have destroyed all your enemies before your
eyes. Now I will make your name as famous as
anyone who has ever lived on the earth!"*

2 Samuel 7:9 NLT

Israel had a long history of conflict. But now that David was established as king, the Lord gave the nation rest from its enemies. David began to dream of building a permanent house for the ark of God, which at that time was kept in a tent. But God told David that one of his offspring would build the temple. David could trust this promise because of God's faithfulness in the past.

The Lord reminded David how "I took you from tending sheep in the pasture and selected you to be the leader of my people Israel" (2 Samuel 7:8 NLT). And then God spoke the words of today's scripture, making sure David knew that he'd always had the divine presence and protection with him.

Though our calling is far different from David's, we can also claim God's power and provision in our lives. Through His Holy Spirit, God actually lives within us—which is why He can say, "I will never abandon you" (Hebrews 13:5 NLT). Jesus has encouraged us to ask His Father for our daily bread, protection from temptation, and forgiveness from sin (Matthew 6:9–13). And we who follow Jesus are assured of ultimate success: "I know the one in whom I trust, and I am sure that he is able to guard what I have entrusted to him until the day of his return" (2 Timothy 1:12 NLT). Our God's trustworthiness gives us courage and hope.

YOU ARE JUSTIFIED

Now it was not written for his sake alone that it was imputed to him, but also for us, to whom it shall be imputed if we believe in Him who raised up Jesus our Lord from the dead, who was delivered for our offenses and was raised again for our justification.

ROMANS 4:23–25 SKJV

Christ was raised from the grave for the justification of all who put their trust in Him, and such are not only pardoned men but justified men. Justification is more than pardon.

It is said of an emperor of Russia that he sent on one occasion for two noblemen who were charged with some conspiracy, and one he found to be perfectly innocent, so he sent him home justified; but the other was proved guilty, yet was pardoned. They both returned to their homes; but ever afterwards they would stand very differently in the estimation of their Sovereign and neighbors. From that may be seen the difference between pardon and justification.

When a man is justified, he can go through the world with his head erect. Satan may come to him and say, "You are a sinner"; but the reply would be, "I know that, but God has forgiven me through Christ."

SEEK GOD, FIND GOD

If you call out for insight and cry aloud
for understanding, if you look for it as for
silver and search for it as for hidden treasure,
then you will understand the fear of the
Lord and find the knowledge of God.

PROVERBS 2:3–5 NIV

In a world where we can have pretty much whatever we want, whenever we want it, it's easy to allow our desires to distract us from the pursuit of the things we truly need. What do we really need? Our hearts and Proverbs 2:5 say, "The knowledge of God."

God created man to have fellowship with Himself. He said, "Let Us make man in Our image, according to Our likeness. . . . And God saw everything that He had made, and behold, it was very good" (Genesis 1:26, 31 skjv).

Our days are filled with many good things. But we often overlook the one most important thing: fellowship, time spent alone with God and His Word. He says that if we seek Him as we would search for silver—if we make Him the real driving force behind everything—*we will find Him*. And when we do, our spiritual bank account will be filled to overflowing.

Jesus doesn't hide from us. In fact, He's standing at the door to your heart right now. In those moments when we feel alone, let's put down what we're doing, give up the selfish ambitions that consume our lives, and open the door to Him.

WHOLEHEARTED FOR THE LORD

*And [Jonah] prayed to the LORD and said, "I ask You,
O LORD, was not this my saying when I was yet in my
country? Therefore I fled before to Tarshish, for I knew
that You are a gracious God, and merciful, slow to anger,
and of great kindness, and repenting of the evil."*

JONAH 4:2 SKJV

In hindsight, Jonah's prayers are pathetic, almost laughable. Apparently it was okay for the Lord to change His mind and spare Jonah's life. But somehow it wasn't all right for God to change His mind and spare the repentant Ninevites.

Granted, Nineveh was wicked. It was the capital of the vicious Assyrian empire, whose soldiers gleefully cut down their enemies. They were even more gleeful and sadistic in torturing their prisoners of war.

Nevertheless, at Jonah's warning, the Assyrian king and his capital city's entire population repented with earnest prayer and serious fasting. How serious? Not even the animals were allowed to eat or drink (Jonah 3:7). And the Lord noticed (Jonah 4:11).

It's ironic that God turned around and used the Assyrians to bring judgment on His own people, the wicked northern kingdom of Israel, a few decades later (2 Kings 15:19–17:23). But not long after that, the Assyrians were more pagan than ever and God was compelled to pronounce a final judgment on Nineveh (see Nahum).

It's been said that God has no grandchildren. Every individual must decide for or against the Lord. Some people choose him halfheartedly, out of fear or social pressure. But those whose hearts are whole find their courage and strength in Him.

A TEAM EFFORT

*So Joshua fought the Amalekites as Moses
had ordered, and Moses, Aaron and Hur went
to the top of the hill. As long as Moses held up his
hands, the Israelites were winning, but whenever
he lowered his hands, the Amalekites were winning.
When Moses' hands grew tired, they took a stone and
put it under him and he sat on it. Aaron and Hur held
his hands up—one on one side, one on the other—so
that his hands remained steady till sunset. So Joshua
overcame the Amalekite army with the sword.*

EXODUS 17:10–13 NIV

Joshua could not complete his task without the work of
Moses. Moses could not support Joshua in his task without
the work of Aaron and Hur. The work was a full day, and
in the end, the task was accomplished. Many times, we
find courage and strength by relying on the help of others.

This was not the first time these men had worked
together. They knew each other's strengths and weaknesses
and were ready to assist when the moment called.

When we encourage our family, coworkers, or fellow
citizens, we more effectively complete tasks and accomplish goals. And the receiving of strength from these same
individuals can help us get past our challenges.

Who is on your team? Or who should be? Reach
out to them, offering and receiving encouragement in
Jesus' name.

VICTORY BELONGS TO GOD

The LORD made David
victorious wherever he went.

2 SAMUEL 8:6 NLT

Saul's dislike of David began shortly after the king appointed the young man as a military commander. Once, as the army returned from a battle victory, women from the towns of Israel came out to meet King Saul, dancing and singing. That was good. But their song elevated David over the king: "Saul has killed his thousands, and David his ten thousands!" (1 Samuel 18:7 NLT). Saul was not happy.

What the king failed to realize was that David's successes on the battlefield had little to do with David himself—but everything to do with God. The Lord was with David, making him victorious wherever he went. The words of today's scripture are repeated in 2 Samuel 8:14.

We know that David wasn't perfect. In fact, later in life, he would commit adultery and ultimately arrange the death of the woman's husband. But he'd been chosen by God to be king and was described as a man after God's own heart (1 Samuel 13:14; Acts 13:22).

All of us have flaws, but God still chooses to work through us. And He empowers us to accomplish what He wills. Keep your focus on the Lord, through prayer and time in His Word. Deny yourself and take up your cross each day (Matthew 16:24). Humbly wait on the Lord and His victory—whatever form that takes.

CHARACTER WINS

Then the presidents and princes sought to find an accusation against Daniel concerning the kingdom, but they could find no accusation or fault, because he was faithful, nor was any error or fault found in him. Then these men said, "We shall not find any accusation against this Daniel unless we find it against him concerning the law of his God."

DANIEL 6:4–5 SKJV

One of the highest eulogies ever paid to a man on earth was pronounced upon Daniel, by his enemies. These men who were connected with the various parts of the kingdom could "find no occasion against this Daniel, except they found it against him concerning the law of his God." What a testimony from his bitterest enemies! Would that it could be said of all of us!

Ah, how his name shines! He had commenced to shine in his early manhood; and he shone right along. Now he is an old man, an old statesman; and yet this is their testimony. There had been no sacrifice of principle to catch votes; no buying up of men's votes or men's consciences. He had walked right straight along.

Character is worth more than anything else in the wide world.

FILLED WITH POWER

But as for me, I am filled with power, with the
Spirit of the LORD, and with justice and might,
to declare to Jacob his transgression, to Israel his sin.
MICAH 3:8 NIV

Micah urged his readers to pay attention to the Lord's warnings of pending judgment. Like his contemporary Isaiah and several other prophets who would come later, Micah repeatedly told God's people to listen. Why? Because their sins were many and their judgment sure.

Like Isaiah, Micah didn't hesitate to denounce the godless rulers, corrupt priests, false prophets, and degenerate people who filled the kingdoms of Israel and Judah (chapters 1–3). Like Isaiah, Micah spoke of days far into the future (chapters 4–5). Like Isaiah, Micah pictured the Lord putting His people on trial (chapter 6). And like Isaiah, Micah contrasted the godlessness of his day with the glorious future ahead (chapter 7).

What inspired Micah to speak out so boldly against the sins of his people? The verse above makes it clear that the Spirit of the Lord gave him the strength.

If God's Spirit lives in us, we too will have the power to speak boldly against injustice and sin—and we'll have the power to deny those sins first in our own lives. We'll be "filled with power" to do whatever it is that God calls us to do.

The key is the indwelling Spirit, which every true Christian possesses, and our conscious, minute-by-minute decision to allow Him to control our lives.

FINDING THE GOOD LIFE

Therefore, I urge you, brothers and sisters, in view of
God's mercy, to offer your bodies as a living sacrifice,
holy and pleasing to God—this is your true and
proper worship. Do not conform to the pattern of this
world, but be transformed by the renewing of your
mind. Then you will be able to test and approve what
God's will is—his good, pleasing and perfect will.

ROMANS 12:1–2 NIV

"You only live once." "Do what feels right." "Find yourself."
These are the popular philosophies of our world.

It's very common to find people pursuing what they
think is best for themselves. But Jesus taught and exem-
plified a much different way.

His life and ministry changed everything. Not only
did Jesus open the pathway to God and eternal life, by
His selfless example He challenged the way we live this
life. "For even the Son of Man did not come to be served,
but to serve," Jesus said, "and to give his life as a ransom
for many" (Mark 10:45 NIV).

In the book of Romans, the apostle Paul likewise
urged Christians to get beyond themselves. Though human
nature is to do whatever feels right in the moment, we
help ourselves by sacrificing our desires to God—serving
Him by building up others, attending to people's needs,
looking after those who cannot look after themselves.

We find the good life by denying our own desires.

THE MORE YOU
STUDY SCRIPTURE. . .

*And when He was alone, those who were around Him
with the twelve asked Him about the parable. And
He said to them, "To you it has been given to know
the mystery of the kingdom of God, but to those who
are outside, all these things are done in parables."*

MARK 4:10–11 SKJV

The Word of God tells us plainly that the natural man
cannot understand spiritual things. It is a spiritual book
and speaks of spiritual things, and a man must be born of
the Spirit before he can understand the Bible. What seems
very dark and mysterious to you now will all be light and
clear when you are born of the Spirit.

I can remember some portions of scripture that were
very dark and mysterious to me when I was converted,
but now they are very clear. I can remember things that
ten years ago were very dark and mysterious, but as I have
gone on I understand them better, and the more we know
of God, and the more we study the Word, the plainer it
will become.

HELP WHEN CORNERED

*But Abishai son of Zeruiah came to David's
rescue and killed the Philistine. Then David's men
declared, "You are not going out to battle with us
again! Why risk snuffing out the light of Israel?"*

2 SAMUEL 21:17 NLT

As David neared the end of his life, he was still going out
to battle with his men. He even fought Philistine giants,
just as he had battled Goliath in his youth. But on one
occasion, David became weak and exhausted from the
fight (2 Samuel 21:15). Ishbi-benob, a descendant of
the giants, carrying a spear with a seven-pound bronze
point, cornered David and was about to kill him. Happily
for the king, help arrived in the form of an Israelite soldier
named Abishai, son of Zeruiah.

We all become battle weary at times. And in some
cases, God doesn't strengthen us personally. Instead, He
helps us face our trial by summoning other believers to our
rescue. Perhaps God does this to humble us—a reminder
of our own frailty will encourage our dependence on Him.
Or maybe He's preparing our rescuer for some even bigger
task in the future.

Are you willing to accept aid from a fellow believer for
the challenges you face? When moments of weariness and
weakness come, don't consider yourself a failure—those
times happen to us all. Instead, thank God for His perfect
wisdom and timing in sending a willing soldier to help
when you're cornered.

WE SHALL BE RICHER

So the LORD blessed the latter end of Job more
than his beginning, for he had fourteen thousand
sheep and six thousand camels and a thousand
yoke of oxen and a thousand female donkeys. He
also had seven sons and three daughters.

JOB 42:12–13 SKJV

We are not all like Job, but we all have Job's God. Though
we have neither risen to Job's wealth, nor will, probably,
ever sink to Job's poverty, yet there is the same God above
us if we be high, and the same God with His everlasting
arms beneath us if we be brought low; and what the Lord
did for Job He will do for us, not precisely in the same
form, but in the same spirit, and with like design.

If, therefore, we are brought low tonight, let us be
encouraged with the thought that God will turn again
our captivity; and let us entertain the hope that after the
time of trial shall be over, we shall be richer, especially in
spiritual things, than ever we were before.

SUPERNATURAL STRENGTH

*"In your strength I [David] can crush an army;
with my God I can scale any wall."*

2 Samuel 22:30 nlt

David was a bundle of contradictions. He was a great sinner who was also a man after God's own heart. He was a man who could be patient but sometimes acted in haste. He showed great mercy—as he did with Jonathan's disabled son, Mephibosheth—or he could be utterly ruthless. He was a warrior as well as a poet. The latter may have made him especially sensitive to understanding who he was before a holy God: a weak vessel.

Three times in 2 Samuel 22, David's song of praise to the Lord, David mentioned that God strengthened him. He sang about God as his rock, his fortress, and his savior. But David didn't stop there. God was his shield, the power that saved him, his place of safety, his refuge, and more.

If the man who killed the giant Goliath recognized his dependence on such a God, how much more should we? We too are bundles of contradictions. We sin much while also chasing after God. We are impatient with others but also try to show compassion. We can only do the good, though, as God works in us.

And once we've tasted of His power, how can we do anything else but praise Him like David did?

FORWARD ON FAITH

When he had finished speaking, he said to Simon, "Now go out where it is deeper, and let down your nets to catch some fish." "Master," Simon replied, "we worked hard all last night and didn't catch a thing. But if you say so, I'll let the nets down again."

LUKE 5:4–5 NLT

Simon, also known as Peter, wasn't a rabbi—he was a fisherman. He didn't tell Jesus how to teach or heal, and he didn't expect Jesus to tell him how to fish. But when Jesus gave him an order, Peter knew enough to listen.

He was about to be schooled.

After Peter followed Jesus' instructions, the fish that evaded him the night before were now lured miraculously into his nets. Soon, Peter and his brother Andrew had to signal another boat to help them with the catch, lest the haul of fish sink their boat. The Gospel writer Luke reports, "When Simon Peter realized what had happened, he fell to his knees before Jesus and said, 'Oh, Lord, please leave me—I'm such a sinful man' " (5:8 NLT).

Peter learned the limits of his own expertise and the faith required to follow the Lord who called him to fish for men.

When we rely on our own expertise—whether we're fishermen, plumbers, businessmen, or evangelists—we aren't depending on God to provide what we truly need. Like Peter, let's admit our own sinfulness and move forward on faith alone.

DO WHAT'S GOOD

He has shown you, O man, what is good. And what
does the LORD require of you, but to do justice and to
love mercy and to walk humbly with your God?
MICAH 6:8 SKJV

Is it true that God has showed mankind what is good?
Yes. Much of the Old Testament—whether by the rules
given to Israel or in the examples of people's lives—clearly
shows what God wants and the danger of doing otherwise.

In the New Testament, did Jesus urge His listeners
"to do justice, and to love mercy and to walk humbly with
your God"? Yes. We can't read far into the Gospels without
seeing things like this: "Love your enemies, bless those
who curse you, do good to those who hate you" (Matthew
5:44 SKJV; see also Luke 6:27, 35) and, "Is it lawful to do
good on the Sabbath day or to do evil, to save life or to
kill?" (Mark 3:4 SKJV; see also Luke 6:9).

Did the apostles say similar things? Yes. Paul taught,
"Therefore, as we have opportunity, let us do good to
all men, especially to those who are of the household of
faith" (Galatians 6:10 SKJV). And Peter wrote, "He who
will love life and see good days, let him refrain his tongue
from evil, and his lips that they do not speak deceit. Let
him turn away from evil and do good. Let him seek peace
and pursue it" (1 Peter 3:10–11 SKJV).

God's expectations are clear: do what's good. He
provides both the desire and the power, which grow as
we exercise each.

GOD'S WEAKNESS?

*For the foolishness of God is wiser than
human wisdom, and the weakness of
God is stronger than human strength.*

1 CORINTHIANS 1:25 NIV

In the Old Testament, the twelve Israelite spies who
explored Canaan agreed that the land was just as God had
described. It flowed with milk and honey (Numbers 13:27).

But there was disagreement on how to proceed. Ten
of the spies said there was no chance of Israel conquering
the land. The people of Canaan were giants and much
stronger than the Israelites, who were like grasshoppers
in comparison.

Two of the spies, though, insisted that God had
promised Canaan to Israel and that made all the difference.
"We should go up and take possession of the land," Caleb
and Joshua said, "for we can certainly do it" (Numbers
13:30 NIV).

The ten fearful spies had forgotten the most significant
thing. God had committed this land to His people, just
as He had committed Himself to them. As the Creator
of everything, as the power behind the plagues on Egypt
and the parting of the Red Sea, He could certainly handle
the inhabitants of Canaan.

God is stronger than any obstacle we could ever face.
In fact, the apostle Paul says God's weakness is stronger
than any human power. His foolishness is wiser than any
human scheming. When we are in God's hands, nothing
should ever frighten us.

LIKE A GOOD SOLDIER

Endure suffering along with me,
as a good soldier of Christ Jesus.

2 TIMOTHY 2:3 NLT

Soldiers go through rigorous training to become battle-ready warriors. They are torn down physically, mentally, and emotionally, then rebuilt into the kind of fighters their country requires. When the actual battle comes, soldiers must endure—it's literally the difference between life and death.

As Christians, we undergo a similar process of training, remaking, and enduring. We were one way before salvation, but we are rebuilt into "good soldier[s] of Christ Jesus." When our spiritual battles come, we—like the apostle Paul—must endure to the end. But where do we get the strength to endure?

In verse 1 (SKJV), Paul tells his protégé Timothy to "be strong in the grace that is in Christ Jesus." We find strength in God's grace, His generous blessing on undeserving people. Grace shows itself in a million ways, but the clearest, most obvious example is Jesus' death on the cross.

If the God of the universe sent His beloved Son as a sacrifice for you, you must be very important to Him. If you are important to God, you can trust that He will take care of you in any and every battle. God's grace allows you to be a "good soldier of Christ Jesus."

WISDOM AND STRENGTH

To fear [the Lord's] name is wisdom.
MICAH 6:9 NIV

Who speaks today's key verse? Obviously, Micah the prophet does, through the inspiration of the Holy Spirit (see 2 Peter 1:21). Job also speaks this truth (Job 28:28). So does the psalmist (Psalm 111:10). In the Proverbs, Solomon says it three times (1:7; 9:10; 15:33). Isaiah puts his own twist on the teaching (Isaiah 11:2; 33:6). In other words, Micah isn't coining a new idea. . .it's a very old and very important truth. So we had best understand and heed it.

There's only one way to be truly wise, and that's by "fearing" the Lord's name. Most people are what the Bible calls "fools," because they have decided they're smart enough to go through life without God. They forget (or choose to ignore the fact) that the Lord is omniscient. . . the reality is that even the most brilliant human being knows only a tiny fraction of what God knows. We can understand only a tiny fraction of His ways.

But today's scripture doesn't focus only on God's omniscience. Notice the mention of His "name"—that is, all of who the Lord is. So our wisdom begins by fearing everything about God, including His omnipotence, His omnipresence, His utter holiness, and His providence and love. The less we know about the Lord, the more we sin. Conversely, the more we know and fear who the Lord is, the wiser we are.

And the wiser we are, the stronger we are—because we'll be strong in His infinite power.

SPEAK WITH AUTHORITY

God gave Solomon very great wisdom and
understanding, and knowledge as vast as the sands
of the seashore. . . . He could speak with authority
about all kinds of plants. . . . He could also speak
about animals, birds, small creatures, and fish.

1 KINGS 4:29, 33 NLT

The Enlightenment period of the seventeenth and eighteenth centuries was grounded in intellectualism. According to *Encyclopedia Britannica*, human reason was heralded as the power "by which humans understand the universe and improve their own condition." But the thinkers of that era had nothing on King Solomon. He received his wisdom from God.

Today, we often hear of highly educated people who don't believe in the triune God. Many argue that Christianity has no place in the public square—that religion is acceptable only if it is kept within the church walls on Sunday mornings. But God cannot be contained like that.

By God's design and grace, Solomon spoke intelligently about the natural sciences. He oversaw the politics, economic policies, and trade of a great nation. He excelled in matters of the mind and the written word.

Sometimes we feel intimidated by the academics, politicians, and business leaders of our world, intelligent and well-educated people who often completely disagree with our biblical morality. But followers of Jesus have "the mind of Christ" (1 Corinthians 2:16 NLT) and the power of the Spirit (Romans 15:13). We can speak with authority on anything God gives us to say.

SPEAK A WORD FOR CHRIST

*. . .praying always with all prayer and supplication
in the Spirit, and watching with all perseverance
and supplication for all saints, and for me, that
words may be given to me, that I may open my
mouth boldly to make known the mystery of the
gospel for which I am an ambassador in chains,
that in it I may speak boldly, as I ought to speak.*
EPHESIANS 6:18–20 SKJV

It is a privilege to work for Jesus; I am tired of hearing about the "duty" of so doing. Oh! If every Christian would resolve not to let a day pass without offering to some individual a personal invitation to come to Christ, in one twelvemonth there would not be a man or a woman in England who would not have heard such an appeal. If Christ died for us, we ought surely to be prepared to speak a word for Him.

I have found this practice has been a great help in keeping my own heart warm. I have felt that my words themselves were cold and icy when I was not working for the salvation of others. There are some who say, "We don't have any sympathy with these special efforts"; and I sympathize with that objection. I believe it is the privilege of the child of God to make continuous efforts for the salvation of others, every day throughout the year.

WHO IS LIKE OUR GOD?

Who is a God like you, who pardons sin and
forgives the transgression of the remnant of his
inheritance? You do not stay angry forever but delight
to show mercy. You will again have compassion
on us; you will tread our sins underfoot and hurl
all our iniquities into the depths of the sea.
MICAH 7:18–19 NIV

From the earliest pages of scripture, we can clearly see
who God is.

The book of Genesis describes Adam and Eve in the
garden of Eden, the serpent's temptation, and humanity's
terrible fall, and then it shows us God's reaction. We see
Him cursing both the serpent and the ground. We read
how He prescribes hard work for men and hard labor in
childbirth for women. But notice that the Lord doesn't
curse Adam and Eve themselves. In His mercy, He sacrifices
an animal or two to make clothing for His beloved people.
In His kindness, the Lord makes it impossible for Adam
and Eve to eat from the tree of life and live forever in a
perpetually fallen world. Instead, He promises a future
Messiah who will tread the serpent underfoot. By this
promise, God is committing Himself—in the person of
Jesus Christ—to die for us and for our sins.

These powerful images of the Lord God—
pardoning, forgiving, showing mercy and compassion,
getting rid of human sin forever—resonate throughout
the rest of scripture.

Who is like our God, indeed!

WISDOM FROM THE SOURCE

Do not deceive yourselves. If any of you think you are wise by the standards of this age, you should become "fools" so that you may become wise. For the wisdom of this world is foolishness in God's sight. As it is written: "He catches the wise in their craftiness."

1 CORINTHIANS 3:18–19 NIV

You're probably familiar with the Old Testament character Daniel and his three friends, Hananiah, Mishael, and Azariah (better known as Shadrach, Meshach, and Abednego). "In every matter of wisdom and understanding about which the king questioned them," Daniel 1:20 reports, "he found them ten times better than all the magicians and enchanters in his whole kingdom" (NIV). The Babylonian king was very pleased with the contributions of these young Jewish exiles. But jealousy burned in the hearts of the native Babylonian "wise men."

The Babylonians consulted with each other. Daniel and his brothers consulted with God. The outcome was dramatically different: Daniel became one of the highest officials in the land, while the wise men and their families were ultimately fed to lions.

This story illustrates what the apostle Paul taught the Corinthians. Wisdom from earthly sources, even the most impressive and respected people, is no match for the wisdom of God.

Our lives are full of choices—some small and insignificant but others life altering. Don't ever think you should make every decision yourself—get your wisdom from the source by seeking God for answers. He will always provide the wisest guidance of all.

FAITH FEEDS ON GOD

For through the grace given to me I say to every man who is among you not to think of himself more highly than he ought to think, but to think soberly, according to the measure of faith God has dealt to every man.

ROMANS 12:3 SKJV

There can be no true prayer without faith; some measure of faith must precede prayer. And yet prayer is also the way to more faith; there can be no higher degree of faith except through much prayer. This is the lesson Jesus teaches here. There is nothing needs so much to grow as our faith.

When Jesus spoke the words, "According to your faith let it be done to you" (Matthew 9:29 SKJV), He announced the law of the kingdom, which tells us that all have not equal degrees of faith, that the same person has not always the same degree, and that the measure of faith must always determine the measure of power and of blessing. If we want to know where and how our faith is to grow, the Master points us to the throne of God.

It is in prayer, in the exercise of the faith I have, in fellowship with the living God, that faith can increase. Faith can only live by feeding on what is divine, on God Himself.

IT WILL BE DONE

*Paul, a servant of God and an apostle of Jesus Christ,
according to the faith of God's elect and the acknowledging
of the truth that is according to godliness, in hope of
eternal life, which God, who cannot lie, promised before
the world began, but has in due times manifested His
word through preaching, which is committed to me
according to the commandment of God our Savior.*

TITUS 1:1–3 SKJV

God is always true to what He promises to do. He made
promises to Abraham, Jacob, Moses, Joshua, etc., and did
He not fulfill them? He will fulfill every word of what He
has promised; yet how few take Him at His word!

When I was a young man I was clerk in the establish-
ment of a man in Chicago, whom I observed frequently
occupied sorting and marking bills. He explained to me
what he had been doing; on some notes he had marked
B, on some D, and on others G; those marked B he told
me were bad, those marked D meant they were doubtful,
and those with G on them meant they were good; and,
said he, you must treat all of them accordingly.

And thus people endorse God's promises, by marking
some as bad and others as doubtful; whereas we ought to
take all of them as good, for He has never once broken
His word, and all that He says He will do, will be done
in the fulness of time.

THE LORD IS OUR STRENGTH

*The LORD is good, a refuge in times of trouble.
He cares for those who trust in him, but with an
overwhelming flood he will make an end of Nineveh.*
NAHUM 1:7–8 NIV

The book of Nahum warns of God's judgment on the Assyrian capital of Nineveh.

Though the entire population of the city had repented of their sins and worshipped the Lord a century earlier (see the book of Jonah), subsequent generations rejected the truth, growing increasingly rebellious, murderous, and vile. As a result, God called the prophet Nahum to pronounce a final judgment on the city.

Its sins included arrogance over its power and wealth, plotting against the Lord God, brutally slaying people without cause, crushing the northern Jewish kingdom of Israel, scheming against the southern kingdom of Judah, and actively promoting the worship of horrid idols.

Over against this wickedness, though, we see the wonderfulness of the Lord our God. He is infinitely and eternally "good"—that's just who He is. He is "a refuge in times of trouble. He cares for those who trust in him"— that is, God is omniscient, omnipresent, and omnipotent, and He loves and protects us.

Nineveh, for all its power, didn't stand a chance against God. The conquering Babylonians so obliterated the Assyrian capital that its location was unknown for twenty-four centuries.

Whatever difficulty you face, the Lord is your strength.

FOREWARNED AND FOREARMED

And David swore moreover and said, "Your father
certainly knows that I have found grace in your eyes,
and he said, 'Do not let Jonathan know this, lest he be
grieved.' But truly, as the LORD lives and as your soul
lives, there is only a step between me and death."

1 SAMUEL 20:3 SKJV

This was David's description of his own condition. King
Saul was seeking to destroy him. The bitter malice of that
king would not be satisfied with anything short of the
blood of his rival.

Jonathan did not know this. He could not believe
so badly of his father as that he could wish to kill the
champion of Israel, the brave, true-hearted young David;
and so he assured David that it could not be so—that he
had not heard of any plots against him.

But David, who knew better, said, "It is certainly
so. Your father seeks my blood, and there is but a step
between me and death." Now it was by knowing his danger that David escaped. Had he remained as ignorant of
his own peril as his friend Jonathan had been, he would
have walked into the lion's mouth, and he would have
fallen by the hand of Saul. But to be forewarned is to
be forearmed; he was, therefore, able to save his life
because he perceived his danger.

GOD STILL PROVIDES

Then the LORD said to Elijah, "Go to the east and hide
by Kerith Brook, near where it enters the Jordan River.
Drink from the brook and eat what the ravens bring
you, for I have commanded them to bring you food."

1 KINGS 17:2–4 NLT

After a series of evil kings had ruled in Israel, God raised
up Elijah the prophet. A drought was on the way, and
God told Elijah to shelter near a brook that fed into the
famed Jordan River. That would provide the prophet's
water. Meanwhile, the Lord was planning to provide
food for Elijah in the most unusual of ways—via ravens.

"If Providence calls us to solitude and retirement, it
becomes us to go: when we cannot be useful, we must be
patient; and when we cannot work for God, we must sit
still quietly for him," Matthew Henry wrote in his classic
commentary. "The ravens were appointed to bring him
meat, and did so. Let those who have but from hand to
mouth, learn to live upon Providence, and trust it for the
bread of the day, in the day."

Sometimes we find ourselves in situations that make
no human sense. But if God calls us to stand on principle,
give generously, love our enemies, or any of a hundred
other things that seem impossible, know that He will
provide for and in our obedience.

Don't hesitate to obey. As He did for Elijah, God still
provides for His people.

WHEN WE'RE DISMAYED

*O L*ORD *my God, my Holy One, you who are*
eternal—surely you do not plan to wipe us out?
*O L*ORD*, our Rock, you have sent these Babylonians*
to correct us, to punish us for our many sins.

HABAKKUK 1:12 NLT

Habakkuk urged his readers to trust the Lord even when evil overran their world. The prophet captured a unique dialogue between himself—the Old Testament's "doubting Thomas"—and God.

How long, Habakkuk asked, would God allow the southern kingdom of Judah to perpetrate wickedness before He judged it (1:1–4)? The Lord replied that He was already raising up the Babylonians to carry the people of Judah into exile (1:5–11).

The answer astonished the prophet. Habakkuk asked how God could plan to use such a vile and pagan nation to judge Judah (1:12–2:1). The Lord replied that He would take care of the Babylonians later. Habakkuk must continue to place his faith in God (2:2–20).

That instruction turns out to be the most important message from the Lord to Habakkuk—and all of us. After all, consider who the Lord is. In the words of today's scripture, He is "my God." He's personal—that's why He could have a dialogue with Habakkuk in the first place. Second, the Lord is "my Holy One, you who are eternal." The Lord is eternally and infinitely holy, just, pure, and righteous. He always does what is right. Finally, He is "our Rock"—that is, to the faithful, not to the obstinate, wicked, and rebellious.

BE A HARD WORKER

We work hard with our own hands. When we
are cursed, we bless; when we are persecuted,
we endure it; when we are slandered, we answer
kindly. We have become the scum of the earth,
the garbage of the world—right up to this moment.

1 Corinthians 4:12–13 niv

Working hard is an admirable trait. Consider the apostle Paul, who worked tirelessly for the gospel of Christ: He spent years on the mission, covering thousands of miles by foot and by boat. He started, encouraged, and corrected churches. Along the way, he wrote several books of the New Testament—much of the time while facing intense persecution.

Paul's work on behalf of Jesus was obvious. But he also labored less visibly to shape his character to be more like his Lord. "I do not run like someone running aimlessly," he told the Corinthian Christians, "I do not fight like a boxer beating the air. No, I strike a blow to my body and make it my slave so that after I have preached to others, I myself will not be disqualified for the prize" (1 Corinthians 9:26–27 niv).

Paul's life and teaching demand that we also work hard, not only outwardly but inwardly. When we do the "heavy lifting" to shape our hearts and minds to become more like Christ, we'll find ourselves stronger when the inevitable troubles of life come on us. We'll be able, like the apostle, to weather our trials with grace.

A MAN IN COMMUNION WITH GOD

And Enoch lived sixty-five years and begot Methuselah.
And Enoch walked with God three hundred years
after he begot Methuselah and begot sons and
daughters. And all the days of Enoch were three
hundred and sixty-five years. And Enoch walked
with God, and he was not, for God took him.

GENESIS 5:21–24 SKJV

Enoch was one of the small number of men against whom nothing is recorded in the Bible. He lived in the midst of the world as Cain and his descendants had made it. In the midst of such a state of things, Enoch "walked with God"; and in the very same world we are also called to walk with God.

The record of his life is that he "had this testimony, that he pleased God" (Hebrews 11:5 SKJV). Notice that this man accomplished nothing that men would call great, but what made him great was that he walked with God.

The faith of Enoch drew God down from heaven to walk with him. He maintained unbroken fellowship with God. A man in communion with God is one of heaven's greatest warriors. He can battle with and overcome the world, the flesh, and the devil.

AN ENDLESS SUPPLY

*"For this is what the LORD, the God of Israel,
says: 'The jar of flour will not be used up and
the jug of oil will not run dry until the day
the LORD sends rain on the land.'"*

1 KINGS 17:14 NIV

Imagine having only enough food in the house for one small meal with your child, knowing it will probably be the last one before you both die of starvation. Then imagine a man that you've never met requesting your food.

That's the scenario a new widow faced in 1 Kings 17. The prophet Elijah arrived in Zarephath (a Gentile city) at the Lord's direction. Also at the Lord's direction, he asked this woman for a meal. She informed him that she didn't have bread—only a little flour and oil.

"Don't be afraid," Elijah told her (verse 13 NIV). Easier said than done, to be sure—but she obeyed, and the Lord was faithful to supply her and her son with food and oil for many days.

It would have been natural to focus on the hardship. And who could have blamed this woman for protecting her last morsels of food for her son? But God's ways of helping people through trials are often much different than we would expect.

Think of an area of your life right now in which you are lacking. Are you willing to offer up what you do have as a sacrifice to God? Pray and ask for His guidance. You might just find that He'll meet your need in a way you never dreamed.

JUST BY FAITH

"The just shall live by his faith."
HABAKKUK 2:4 SKJV

Today's scripture is quoted three times by New Testament writers, in Romans 1:17, Galatians 3:11, and Hebrews 10:38. This verse must have something important to say to us.

The word *just* speaks of someone who is humble, fully dependent on the Lord God, and living righteously according to His Word. These three characteristics cannot exist independently. You can't be humble while relying on your own strength and intelligence. Nor can you fully depend on the Lord while ignoring and disobeying the Bible. These characteristics are bound together inseparably.

The word *faith* speaks of one's belief and trust in the Lord and of his steadiness in revering and obeying Him. "Faith" isn't something in the past—it's something that directly shapes what you think, feel, say, and do today. Faith, then, is a way of life borne out of humility, wholehearted dependence on the Lord, and righteous living according to scripture.

Any of us can claim to be humble, just, and righteous, but often we're not. How can we be sure we're just and living by faith?

Jesus said it best: "Everyone who hears these words of mine and puts them into practice is like a wise man who built his house on the rock" (Matthew 7:24 NIV). Know what He wants of you, by studying His Word. Then do what it says. It's the only way to really live. . .just by faith.

TAKE IT TO THE LORD

So he got up and ate and drank. Strengthened by
that food, he traveled forty days and forty nights
until he reached Horeb, the mountain of God.

1 KINGS 19:8 NIV

Living for the one true God has always been risky. It often comes with a cost. Jesus explains why: "People loved darkness instead of light because their deeds were evil" (John 3:19 NIV).

Rather than repenting, those who love darkness often turn to persecution. Elijah experienced that after executing the 450 prophets of Baal, prompting Jezebel—the wife of King Ahab—to threaten to kill God's prophet.

Elijah ran for his life. When he came to Beersheba of Judah, he sat under a juniper tree and asked the Lord to take his life. Exhausted, Elijah fell asleep, only to be awakened and fed by an angel. Perhaps still depressed, Elijah fell back asleep until the angel repeated his actions. Elijah gained a miraculous strength that lasted forty days and forty nights.

Have you ever reached the end of your strength? Run out of resolve to serve the Lord? Sometimes the challenge is just too difficult, and everything seems to be against you. When you feel like Elijah (you just want to give up), pray like Elijah (tell the Lord exactly how you feel). Admit that you are drained, frightened, and unable to face the challenge in your own strength. This is the precise moment when God takes over, providing courage and strength to sustain you.

PRAY WISELY

The LORD is in his holy temple;
let all the earth be silent before him.

HABAKKUK 2:20 NIV

Ecclesiastes 3:7 tells us that there is "a time to be silent and a time to speak" (NIV). In Habakkuk's prophecy, we see both in action.

In 1:13, God was asked to break His silence and speak to Habakkuk. But in 2:20, Habakkuk told everyone to be silent before the Lord.

Woe to us when God doesn't speak; on the other hand, woe to us if we don't stop speaking to Him! Jesus taught, "When you pray, do not keep on babbling like pagans, for they think they will be heard because of their many words" (Matthew 6:7 NIV).

Does this mean we should never offer lengthy prayers to the Lord? No. Solomon, who encouraged "few words" in Ecclesiastes 5, also offered a substantial prayer at the dedication of God's temple (1 Kings 8:22–53; 2 Chronicles 6:12–42). And Jesus, shortly before His arrest and crucifixion, prayed the long "high priestly prayer" in Gethsemane (John 17:1–26).

The difference seems to be respect. Our unthinking babbling neither honors God nor helps us. But a reasoned prayer that acknowledges His holiness and requests His blessing will always reach God's heart. With the right frame of mind, we can "approach God's throne of grace with confidence" and "receive mercy and find grace to help us in our time of need" (Hebrews 4:16 NIV).

159

TRAIN HARD

Do you not know that in a race all the runners run,
but only one gets the prize? Run in such a way as to get
the prize. Everyone who competes in the games goes into
strict training. They do it to get a crown that will not
last, but we do it to get a crown that will last forever.

1 Corinthians 9:24–25 niv

Just as a marathon runner would not wait until race day to prepare, we as Christians cannot wait for adversity to strike before we make plans to deal with it. In those moments when life is going well, we can arm ourselves for future battles by spending time in prayer, memorizing scripture, and sharpening our faith in fellowship with Christian friends.

Jesus tells His twelve disciples (and, by extension, we as Christians today) that there will be trouble in life (John 16:33). The fact is that we could find ourselves engaged in a spiritual battle at any moment.

That's why we must be diligent to prepare, engaging in the training that Paul describes in 1 Corinthians 9. As we work to strengthen our relationship with God, challenging our minds and bodies to behave more like Christ, we are developing courage and strength for our trials. When trouble rears its ugly head, our rigorous preparation will put us in good stead—not just to survive, but to win.

OPEN EYES

And Elisha prayed, "Open his eyes, LORD,
so that he may see." Then the LORD opened the
servant's eyes, and he looked and saw the hills full
of horses and chariots of fire all around Elisha.
2 KINGS 6:17 NIV

As Syria and Israel fought a war, the prophet Elisha was able
to inform the king of Israel about all of Syria's movements.
When the Syrian leader got wind of Elisha's actions, he sent
troops to capture him in Dothan. Elisha's servant woke
up the next morning and saw they were surrounded. But
Elisha explained that the Syrians were outnumbered. He
prayed a simple prayer and his servant's eyes were opened
to see that all around them were horses and chariots of fire.

Elisha's servant could only see trouble with his physical
eyes. Then, in answer to the prophet's prayer, the Lord
opened the servant's spiritual eyes to the larger reality.
Elisha understood what the apostle Paul would write centuries later: "Our struggle is not against flesh and blood,
but against the rulers, against the authorities, against the
powers of this dark world and against the spiritual forces
of evil in the heavenly realms" (Ephesians 6:12 NIV).

Spiritual battles are being fought all around us. Satan
wants to steer us off track, making us think that other
people are our enemies—or our salvation. Pray today for
the spiritual eyes to see God's reality: He has the power to
protect and prevail in any danger you encounter.

NO MATTER WHAT, LOOK TO GOD

"Although the fig tree shall not blossom, fruit shall not be on the vines, the labor of the olive shall fail, the fields shall yield no food, the flock shall be cut off from the fold, and there shall be no herd in the stalls, yet I will rejoice in the LORD. I will rejoice in the God of my salvation. The LORD God is my strength, and He will make my feet like deer's feet, and He will make me walk on my high places."

HABAKKUK 3:17–19 SKJV

Habakkuk concludes his prophecy with a hauntingly beautiful psalm. The closing lines, quoted above, speak of terrible challenges—yet also the experience of the Lord's strength.

Like many other prophets, Habakkuk served a people who had sinned greatly against God. And when the Lord sent punishment by way of the powerful Babylonian army, Judah's orchards, vineyards, fields, flocks, and herds were wiped out. There was little food left for the poor, devastated remnant of God's people. Physically, what could be worse?

But after the shock of the invasion, Habakkuk focused his attention on the Lord. After all, God is the source of everything, from our daily physical needs to our emotional and spiritual strength to our eternal salvation. This recognition explains Habakkuk's otherwise inexplicable joy. The prophet was so energized by the Lord that he imagined himself climbing the surrounding mountains like a sure-footed deer.

In this life, trials are guaranteed. But so is God's presence and strength for those willing to seek them. No matter what, look to God. You'll find Him.

ACCEPT HELP

"One man from each tribe, each of them the head of his family, is to help you. These are the names of the men who are to assist you."

NUMBERS 1:4–5 NIV

The fourth book of the Old Testament begins with a census, hence the name *Numbers*. In the Sinai Desert, fourteen months after the Israelites left their slavery in Egypt, God told Moses to count the Israelite men "who are twenty years old or more and able to serve in the army" (Numbers 1:3 NIV). It was a big job, since that number ultimately came out to 603,550!

But Moses didn't have to count each of these potential soldiers himself. That would have been nearly impossible, finding each eligible male among a nomadic nation of perhaps two million or more people. God specifically told Moses to call on the help of twelve men, the current heads of the various tribes of Israel: Elizur from the tribe of Reuben, Shelumiel from the tribe of Simeon, Nahshon from the tribe of Judah, and on down the line. Considering that, on average, these men were counting some fifty thousand military-age males themselves, it's safe to assume that they too called on help to accomplish their task.

Many men hate to ask for help—or even to accept it when offered. But scripture contains many examples of people working together, whether on a physical job or an emotional and spiritual level. Strength and courage for life often come through our fellow believers.

THE LORD'S FAVOR

Then Jehoahaz sought the LORD's favor,
and the LORD listened to him.

2 KINGS 13:4 NIV

In the Old Testament, we often see the kings of both Israel and Judah failing to fully follow the Lord's commands and subsequently paying a heavy price for their sin. It's easy to wonder why they weren't more faithful. Couldn't they see that their way led to destruction? Couldn't they understand that God wanted the best for them and their people? Of course, we have the benefit of scripture and hindsight—but don't we often act in the same ways?

Jehoahaz ruled for seventeen years in Israel and he—as so many others before him—did evil. So the anger of the Lord burned against Israel, and they ended up oppressed by the Syrians. But when Jehoahaz begged for the Lord's favor, God listened to him. And the Lord saved His people from their enemy.

Sometimes we find ourselves in challenging situations of our own making, sometimes due to carelessness and sometimes due to conscious sin. When that happens, don't ever succumb to the lie that you are too far gone for the Lord. He always cares and will act on behalf of a humble heart. That's why the Bible often shows Him rescuing disobedient kings.

Of course, it's far better to walk in obedience. But if you stray and find yourself in the proverbial pigpen, never hesitate to call out to the Lord. He is ready to show favor.

FEEDING THE MULTITUDE

Then He took the five loaves and the two fish,
and looking up to heaven, He blessed them, and broke
them, and gave to the disciples to set before the multitude.
And they all ate and were filled, and twelve baskets of
fragments that remained were taken up by them.

LUKE 9:16–17 SKJV

Jesus' twelve apostles were on a mission to preach and heal in Jewish communities around the Sea of Galilee. When they returned, they inadvertently brought a crowd of thousands of people with them. While the disciples wanted to send the crowd away, Jesus had compassion on the people—and saw a teachable moment for His team.

With echoes of the forthcoming Last Supper, Jesus took the bread, blessed it, broke it, and gave it to the disciples. They distributed what He had given them, and what was originally deemed insufficient ended in twelve baskets of leftovers.

For the crowd who ate the bread, Jesus' act cast Him in the light of Moses who prayed and provided manna for God's people. This was truly a prophet!

For the disciples who doubted their resources, Jesus showed that it is not the amount of bread or fish (or human ability) that enables the feeding of a multitude, but faith in the God of infinite resources. This was truly the Messiah!

When we feel our ability insufficient for the task God has given us, He asks us to move forward in faith—not in our strength but in His. Do as Jesus did: pray for blessing, break the bread, and trust in God's ability to provide.

GOD, THE MIGHTY WARRIOR

*The great day of the LORD is near—near and
coming quickly. The cry on the day of the LORD
is bitter; the Mighty Warrior shouts his battle cry.*

ZEPHANIAH 1:14 NIV

The prophet Zephaniah described God as a "Mighty
Warrior," shouting a battle cry on the "great day of the
LORD." This latter phrase speaks of God's terrifying judg-
ments both near at hand and far into the future, both on
God's people and the surrounding pagan nations.

During the reign of King Josiah, Zephaniah warned
of God's judgment against Judah. The nation's sins
included idolatry, child sacrifice, pride, and indifference
to the things of the Lord. The nations of Philistia, Moab,
Ammon, Ethiopia, and Assyria would also suffer God's
heavy punishment.

But if the people would turn from their sins, they
would find the Mighty Warrior on their side. "Seek the
LORD, all you humble of the land, you who do what he
commands," Zephaniah told Judah. "Seek righteousness,
seek humility; perhaps you will be sheltered on the day
of the LORD's anger" (Zephaniah 2:3 NIV). There would
even be blessing on the other side (3:10–20).

As Christians, possessors of God's Holy Spirit, we
enjoy a more intimate relationship with this powerful
God than the ancient Jews did. Whatever battles we
face—from outside or within—God, the Mighty Warrior,
is on our side.

A WAY OUT

*So, if you think you are standing firm, be careful
that you don't fall! No temptation has overtaken you
except what is common to mankind. And God is
faithful; he will not let you be tempted beyond what
you can bear. But when you are tempted, he will
also provide a way out so that you can endure it.*

1 Corinthians 10:12–13 niv

Some biblical principles must be extrapolated from multiple passages that only touch on a topic. Then there are biblical promises that hit you between the eyes. The thirteenth verse of 1 Corinthians 10 is one of the latter.

When we are tempted, God will provide a way of escape. Not *might*, not *could*, but *will*. That is a guarantee of strength for the dangers of sin.

What's not guaranteed is our own obedience. Will we walk away when the temptation comes? Will we tell ourselves "no" when our emotions are saying "yes"? As difficult as it may seem to resist the lure of sin, we have God's promise that we will never "be tempted beyond what [we] can bear."

Maybe it's worth memorizing these verses, so the Holy Spirit can bring them to mind at the appropriate moment. Temptation is a normal human experience. But, biblically speaking, there is no reason for it ever to lead to sin.

WASHED IN THE BLOOD OF THE LAMB

For when we were still without strength, in due time
Christ died for the ungodly. For one will scarcely die for
a righteous man, yet perhaps for a good man some would
even dare to die. But God demonstrates His love toward
us, in that while we were still sinners, Christ died for us.
ROMANS 5:6–8 SKJV

Many people try to come to Christ but think they cannot come unless they first become good. But Jesus loves His people even before their sins are washed away. He loves them and then washes them in His own blood, as it is written, "To Him who loved us and washed us from our sins in His own blood, and has made us kings and priests to God and His Father, to Him be glory and dominion forever and ever. Amen" (Revelation 1:5–6 SKJV).

Oh! It is wonderful love. To think that He loves them first and then washes them in His blood free from their sins! There is no devil in hell that can pluck them out of His hand. They are perfectly safe, for they are washed in the blood of the Lamb.

FOCUS ON THE ETERNAL

Therefore we do not lose heart. Though outwardly
we are wasting away, yet inwardly we are being
renewed day by day. For our light and momentary
troubles are achieving for us an eternal glory that
far outweighs them all. So we fix our eyes not on
what is seen, but on what is unseen, since what is
seen is temporary, but what is unseen is eternal.

2 CORINTHIANS 4:16–18 NIV

Why were the early Christians so persistent? How could they go to such great lengths for their faith, when their actions often brought persecution and even death?

The reason is simple, actually: Their focus was not on the pain and trouble of the present, or even of the remaining years of this life. Instead, their eyes were on their eternal future with Jesus Christ. This is the view that we today can and should take.

No matter what trials and hardships we face, Jesus is worth it. Our brief, passing life—what the book of James calls "a mist" (James 4:14 NIV)—is only a microscopic bit of our entire experience. This life is not the end for followers of Jesus! And that is why Paul did not lose heart. That is why we do not need to lose heart.

Whatever troubles we face today will mean nothing compared to the eternal life of joy we'll one day share with our Lord.

LAY HOLD OF THE ALTAR

*Then news came to Joab, for Joab had turned after
Adonijah, though he had not turned after Absalom.
And Joab fled to the tabernacle of the LORD and
took hold of the horns of the altar. . . . And Benaiah
came to the tabernacle of the LORD and said to him,
"This is what the king says: 'Come forth.'" And
he said, "No, but I will die here." And Benaiah
brought word to the king again, saying, "This is
what Joab said and what he answered me."*

1 KINGS 2:28, 30 SKJV

I have two lessons which I am anxious to teach at this
time. The first is derived from the fact that Joab found
no benefit of sanctuary even though he laid hold upon
the horns of the altar of God's house, from which I gather
this lesson—that outward ordinances will avail nothing.
Before the living God, who is greater and wiser than
Solomon, it will be of no avail to any man to lay hold
upon the horns of the altar.

But, second, there is an altar—a spiritual altar—
whereof if a man do but lay hold upon the horns and
say, "Nay; but I will die here," he shall never die; but he
shall be safe against the sword of justice forever; for the
Lord has appointed an altar in the person of His own
dear Son, Jesus Christ, where there shall be shelter for the
very vilest of sinners if they do but come and lay hold
thereon.

DELIVER US!

"Now, LORD our God, deliver us from his hand,
so that all the kingdoms of the earth may
know that you alone, LORD, are God."
2 KINGS 19:19 NIV

Sennacherib, king of Assyria, couldn't imagine that Israel's God was any stronger than the gods of the other nations he'd conquered.

"Has the god of any nation ever delivered his land from the hand of the king of Assyria?" Sennacherib taunted. "Where are the gods of Hamath and Arpad? Where are the gods of Sepharvaim, Hena and Ivvah? Have they rescued Samaria from my hand? Who of all the gods of these countries has been able to save his land from me? How then can the LORD deliver Jerusalem from my hand?" (2 Kings 18:33–35 NIV).

Sennacherib soon found out how wrong he was. An angel of the Lord killed 185,000 Assyrians (2 Kings 19:35). God did so for His name's sake (2 Kings 19:34).

Who or what is your Assyria? It probably seems insurmountable in your own strength. But, praise God, you don't have to rely on your own strength. Like King Hezekiah in today's scripture, go to the Lord in prayer. If He delivers you, praise Him publicly, so everyone else can know God's power and strength. If He allows you to go through a trial, praise Him anyway, and rely on His strength to endure. Either way, God is worthy of your worship.

REWARD TO COME

"For whoever wants to save their life will lose it,
but whoever loses their life for me will save it."

Luke 9:24 niv

The apostles knew that Jesus was the Messiah. He taught with power. He performed miracles like the prophets of old. But the twelve didn't understand the kind of messiah Jesus was to be.

Everyone in Israel was waiting and hoping for the Son of Man promised in Daniel 7:13–14 (niv): "In my vision at night I looked, and there before me was one like a son of man, coming with the clouds of heaven. He approached the Ancient of Days and was led into his presence. He was given authority, glory and sovereign power; all nations and peoples of every language worshiped him. His dominion is an everlasting dominion that will not pass away, and his kingdom is one that will never be destroyed."

When Jesus came to earth, Israel was subject to Roman authority. Jews longed for the Messiah to come in power and might, to be King over every nation, to throw off the chains of Roman rule. But Jesus was a different kind of messiah.

To save the world, He had to die. His coronation would be with a crown of thorns. And everyone who followed Him could expect the same treatment. If we want to live, we must lay aside our selfish desires—even our instinct for self-preservation. We must die to this life to be filled with Christ's life.

Jesus never promised wealth or power for His followers in this life. The reward is in the eternal life to follow.

"I AM WITH YOU"

*Then Zerubbabel son of Shealtiel, Joshua son of Jozadak,
the high priest, and the whole remnant of the people
obeyed the voice of the LORD their God and the message
of the prophet Haggai, because the LORD their God had
sent him. And the people feared the LORD. Then Haggai,
the LORD's messenger, gave this message of the LORD
to the people: "I am with you," declares the LORD.*

HAGGAI 1:12–13 NIV

The prophet Haggai urged his readers to repent of their
misplaced priorities. He was the first of three prophets
to rebuke God's people after the Babylonian captivity.
Although more than fifty thousand had forsaken their
idolatrous ways, returned to the land of Judah, and started
to rebuild the temple, they had not wholeheartedly committed themselves to serving God.

Eventually, their work on the temple foundation
stopped. Years went by with no progress. Meanwhile,
drought crippled their agriculture. "You have planted
much, but harvested little," God told them. "You eat, but
never have enough" (Haggai 1:6 NIV).

The Lord exhorted the people and their leaders to
consider their miserable plight and get back to work on
the temple, and the people listened. And when they heard
and obeyed, God made one of the most beautiful promises
in all of scripture: "I am with you."

YOU MATTER

If the foot says, "I am not a part of the body because
I am not a hand," that does not make it any less a
part of the body. And if the ear says, "I am not part
of the body because I am not an eye," would that
make it any less a part of the body? If the whole body
were an eye, how would you hear? Or if your whole
body were an ear, how would you smell anything?

1 CORINTHIANS 12:15–17 NLT

Herding the Corinthian Christians into one cohesive group
was a significant challenge for the apostle Paul. There was
pride and prejudice in the congregation, with various
factions claiming to follow Paul, Apollos, Peter, and (the
really spiritual ones) Jesus. Some church members were
taking others to court. People in the church were allowing
one particular member to live in gross sexual sin.

Toward the end of his first letter to Corinth, in what we
now call 1 Corinthians 12, Paul tried to explain how every
member played an important—really, indispensable—
role in the church, the "body of Christ." Whether they were
eyes or ears or feet or hands, each Christian in Corinth
had God-given responsibilities and privileges. Each one of
them mattered, both to God and to their fellow believers.

Wherever this scripture finds you today, remember
that there are no spare parts in the body of Christ. No one
is more important than another, and no one is insignificant.
You matter—so do the job God gave you!

JOINT HEIRS WITH JESUS

And He who sat on the throne said, "Behold, I make all things new." And He said to me, "Write, for these words are true and faithful." And He said to me, "It is done. I am Alpha and Omega, the beginning and the end. To him who is thirsty I will freely give of the fountain of the water of life. He who overcomes shall inherit all things, and I will be his God, and he shall be My son."

REVELATION 21:5–7 SKJV

After the Chicago fire a man came up to me and said in a sympathizing tone, "I understand you lost everything, Moody, in the Chicago fire."

"Well, then," said I, "someone has misinformed you."

"Indeed! Why I was certainly told you had lost all."

"No; it is a mistake," I said, "quite a mistake."

"Have you got much left, then?" asked my friend.

"Yes," I replied, "I have got much more left than I lost; though I cannot tell how much I have lost."

"Well, I am glad of it, Moody; I did not know you were that rich before the fire."

"Yes," said I, "I am a good deal richer than you could conceive; and here is my title-deed: 'He that overcometh shall inherit all things.' " They say the Rothschilds cannot tell how much they are worth; and that is just my case. All things in the world are mine; I am joint heir with Jesus the Son of God.

DEATH ISN'T THE END

"Go back and tell Hezekiah, the ruler of my people,
'This is what the LORD, the God of your father
David, says: I have heard your prayer and
seen your tears; I will heal you.'"

2 KINGS 20:5 NIV

King Hezekiah's illness seemed to come out of the blue. . .and it was terminal. The Lord told the faithful king to put his house in order because he wasn't going to recover. Hezekiah did what any of us would do: he prayed. Oddly, though, he didn't pray directly for healing.

"Remember, LORD," he said, "how I have walked before you faithfully and with wholehearted devotion and have done what is good in your eyes" (2 Kings 20:3 NIV). In other words, Hezekiah "reminded" God that he had lived in a way that seemed worthy of a *longer* life. He'd been as faithful to God as a man could be. The Lord graciously heard Hezekiah's prayer and granted him an additional fifteen years.

Hezekiah was facing what we will all face someday—mortality. Most of us don't really want to think about our own deaths, but when we follow Jesus, our mortality should hold no terror. No matter how long we live, we are destined to die, and for believers, the Lord alone is our goal (see Psalm 16:5). Do not fear. Death isn't the end for us as believers—it's simply the beginning of a perfect, sinless, everlasting life.

THE LORD'S ALMIGHTY, SO BE STRONG

"'Now be strong, Zerubbabel,' declares the LORD.
'Be strong, Joshua son of Jozadak, the high priest. Be strong,
all you people of the land,' declares the LORD, 'and work.
For I am with you,' declares the LORD Almighty. . . .
The glory of this present house will be greater than the glory
of the former house,' says the LORD Almighty. 'And in this
place I will grant peace,' declares the LORD Almighty."

HAGGAI 2:4, 9 NIV

God gave the prophet Haggai several messages for the leaders and people of Judah. In Haggai 2, the Lord urged them to be strong even though their task of rebuilding the Jerusalem temple was arduous (verses 1–9).

In today's key verses, we can't miss the threefold repetition of one of God's favorite names: "the LORD Almighty." He is the omnipotent and all-powerful God! And still that is only a part of His infinite personality.

We also can't miss the threefold repetition of the command, "be strong." Through Haggai, God told His people to be courageous and brave. This is the same command the Lord gave to Joshua and many other heroes of the faith in both the Old and New Testaments. The Lord even told the normally fearless apostle Paul, "Do not be afraid; keep on speaking, do not be silent. For I am with you" (Acts 18:9–10 NIV). That final phrase is yet another biblical favorite, as we see in Haggai 2:4 above.

What does all this mean to us? If we forget that the Lord is almighty, we won't be strong. When we acknowledge God's immense power, we can accomplish whatever He calls us to do.

STOP AND REMEMBER

And the LORD spoke to Moses in the wilderness of Sinai, in the first month of the second year after they had come out of the land of Egypt, saying, "Let the children of Israel also keep the Passover at its appointed season."
NUMBERS 9:1–2 SKJV

One year removed from their miraculous escape from Egypt, God told the Israelites to observe the Passover, "according to all its rites and according to all its ceremonies" (Numbers 9:3 SKJV). Those rites and ceremonies are explained in Exodus 12, which also describes the death of the Egyptian firstborn, the ultimate plague that caused Pharaoh to let God's people go.

Now in the wilderness, on their way to the promised land of Canaan, the people were to stop and remember how God had rescued them from their slavery. Ideally, this recollection would strengthen them for the challenges of their journey and the settlement of Canaan. Sadly, from our perspective, we realize the people were only *one-fortieth* of their way home. The Israelites complained and feared and distrusted God, and nearly every one died in the wilderness. Different generations, decades later, would enter the promised land.

As Christians, we have an advantage the ancient Israelites lacked: God's Spirit living within us. But we're still prone to complain and fear and distrust God, so the directive to Israel is a good one for us too: stop and remember.

What good things has God done in your life? What miracles, even? The memories of His goodness and strength can help you through every challenge today.

START FRESH

*"Go, inquire of the LORD for me and for the people
and for all Judah concerning the words of this book
that has been found, for great is the wrath of the
LORD that is kindled against us because our fathers
have not listened to the words of this book, to do
according to all that is written concerning us."*

2 KINGS 22:13 SKJV

Much had changed since good King Hezekiah's reign.
His son, Manasseh, did evil in the Lord's sight. So did
Manasseh's son, Amon. By the time Amon's son, Josiah,
became king at age eight, the book of the law had long since
faded from Judah's memory. It wasn't till the eighteenth
year of Josiah's reign that the high priest stumbled across
the Law in the temple. He took it to the king.

After hearing the law read, Josiah tore his clothes in
mourning. He realized that God's wrath was on the nation
because it had neglected His Word. But because Josiah's
heart was responsive, God relented—at least for a while.

If your Bible has been gathering dust, change that
today. Crack it open and begin to read. Praise God,
Christians today are under the covenant of grace—one
that is far superior to the rules of the Old Testament.
But there's a principle in Josiah's story that still applies to
us today: As we stray from the Word, we're sowing troubled seeds that yield a difficult harvest. As we return to
scripture, it will mold and shape us into the image of
Christ. How could we be more blessed?

FREEDOM IN CHRIST

*To the Jews who had believed him, Jesus said,
"If you hold to my teaching, you are really
my disciples. Then you will know the truth,
and the truth will set you free."*

John 8:31–32 niv

Everyone serves a master. We are all slaves to someone (or something). The implications of this teaching were uncomfortable to the Jews Jesus originally addressed. They're uncomfortable to us today.

When Jesus told a crowd how they could be free, they balked. "We are Abraham's descendants and have never been slaves of anyone," they argued. "How can you say that we shall be set free?" (John 8:33 niv).

They apparently forgot the Jews' slavery experience in Egypt; how Israel had been conquered by Assyrian, Babylonian, Persian, and Syrian armies; and how they were currently subject to Roman authority. Long-term slavery had seemingly convinced them that they had never been slaves at all. Who was Jesus to offer them freedom?

But Jesus was qualified to offer freedom, because He was the only one who never served an earthly master!

Today, we are faced with the same proposition of freedom. By holding to Jesus' teachings—including the hard ones like self-sacrifice and loving our neighbors—we prove ourselves to be His disciples. When Jesus is our Master, we are free from the world's slavery.

Freedom in Christ does not mean we can do whatever we want. We are free to do what *God* wants—and are given the courage to accomplish His tasks.

RETURN TO GOD

"Therefore tell the people: This is what the LORD Almighty says: 'Return to me,' declares the LORD Almighty, 'and I will return to you,' says the LORD Almighty."

ZECHARIAH 1:3 NIV

One mystery of the Christian life is why followers of Jesus would ever stray away from God. And yet that's not only possible but common. Even the great apostle Paul said, "I do not understand what I do. For what I want to do I do not do, but what I hate I do. . . . The evil I do not want to do—this I keep on doing" (Romans 7:15, 19 NIV). Paul blamed the problem on the "sin living in me" (verse 20 NIV).

As Christians, most of us know the promise of 1 John 1:9—"If we confess our sins, he is faithful and just and will forgive us our sins and purify us from all unrighteousness" (NIV). Or, to paraphrase Zechariah, "Return to God and He will return to you."

Sin weakens us. It makes us slaves to Satan, a power far less than God but far greater than ourselves. When we continue in sin, we're like shackled prisoners being marched down a road not of our own choosing.

But like the father in Jesus' story of the prodigal son, God is waiting for us to come to our senses (Luke 15:17). When we decide to turn away from sin and back to God, He comes running to meet us. And there's no better place to be than in His will.

BETTER DAYS ARE COMING

*Our earthly bodies are planted in the ground
when we die, but they will be raised to live forever.
Our bodies are buried in brokenness, but they will be
raised in glory. They are buried in weakness, but they
will be raised in strength. They are buried as natural
human bodies, but they will be raised as spiritual bodies.*

1 CORINTHIANS 15:42–44 NLT

No matter how hard this life becomes, Christians can look forward to better days ahead.

In this world, our bodies become weary, old, and sick. Our emotions can swing from joy to misery with a quick turn of circumstances. Whether we always realize it or not, we are engaged in a cosmic spiritual battle against the sworn enemy of God. "People are born for trouble," the Old Testament character Job noted, "as readily as sparks fly up from a fire" (5:7 NLT).

That's the bad news. But God is the author of good news, the meaning of the word *gospel*. When we believe in the work of His Son, Jesus Christ, we are placed on an upward path. There will still be aches and pains and sorrows and tears in this world, ending in the decline and death of our bodies. But the apostle Paul promises that death is only the gateway to real life.

When life is hard—when it's tough to get out of bed, when there seems to be no light at the end of the proverbial tunnel—remember that better days are coming. Someday, you'll be "raised to live forever. . .in glory. . .in strength." If you follow Jesus Christ, this is your eternal destiny.

NOT LOOKING AT OUR FAULTS

So the LORD blessed the latter end of Job more
than his beginning. . . . After this, Job lived
a hundred and forty years and saw his sons
and his sons' sons, even four generations.
So Job died, being old and full of days.
JOB 42:12, 16–17 SKJV

The story of Job has a happy ending. Skeptics may dismiss the entire narrative, but for those who know—beyond a shadow of a doubt—that every word of God is true, this ending is confirmation of the true nature of God and the faithfulness of Jesus Christ.

There are no easy answers to the question of why bad things happen to good people. But the Bible says *no one* is good, really. We have all sinned and fallen short of the glory of God. These things were true of Job as well. But still, God said of Job, "There is none like him on the earth, a perfect and an upright man, one who fears God and turns away from evil" (Job 1:8 SKJV).

As shocking as it may seem, God is not looking at our faults. Are they there? Of course. But when we say yes to Jesus Christ, when we ask Him to come and make our heart His home, those sins are cast as far away as the east is from the west (see Psalm 103:12).

Job was blessed at the end of his life because God loved him just as He loves us. And God's promise is to bless us and provide for all our needs as well—when we love and trust Him with all our heart.

COMMIT TO GOD'S TRUTH

*But you, dear friends, by building yourselves up in
your most holy faith and praying in the Holy Spirit,
keep yourselves in God's love as you wait for the mercy
of our Lord Jesus Christ to bring you to eternal life.*

JUDE 20–21 NIV

The New Testament letter of Jude bears some striking similarities to 2 Peter. Jude—believed by many to be a half brother of Jesus (see Matthew 13:55 and Mark 6:3)—actually quoted Peter in verses 17 and 18: "But, dear friends, remember what the apostles of our Lord Jesus Christ foretold. They said to you, 'In the last times there will be scoffers who will follow their own ungodly desires'" (NIV; see 2 Peter 3:3). And Jude made several other allusions found in the second chapter of 2 Peter: about the imprisonment of fallen angels; the destruction of Sodom and Gomorrah; proud sinners who speak evil of "celestial beings," and false teachers and their condemnation. Jude even echoed some of Peter's descriptions of false teachers: compare "mists driven by a storm" (2 Peter 2:17 NIV) and "clouds without rain, blown along by the wind" (Jude 12 NIV).

Some might accuse Jude of plagiarism. But we can assume that God was simply directing Jude to confirm and fortify the important message Peter had shared.

False teaching destroys lives. Careful study, good doctrine, and obedience to God's Word make us strong, ready for any and every attack of the world, the flesh, and the devil. We can, as Jude urges in today's scripture, build ourselves up in the faith and keep ourselves in God's love. But to do so, we must commit ourselves to God's truth.

ONE OF GOD'S PEOPLE

"Shout and be glad, Daughter Zion. For I am coming, and I will live among you," declares the LORD. "Many nations will be joined with the LORD in that day and will become my people."

ZECHARIAH 2:10–11 NIV

Chances are, most men reading this devotional do not have a Jewish heritage. God's historic people make up only a tiny percentage of the world population.

But even though the Old Testament is largely the story of God choosing a man (Abraham) and making a special nation of his family (Israel), there are also indicators that one day everyone will have an opportunity to become one of God's people. Today's scripture, from the prophet Zechariah, is a case in point.

While the recently exiled Jews were rebuilding the temple in Jerusalem, God promised His presence and protection, saying, "Whoever touches you touches the apple of [My] eye" (Zechariah 2:8 NIV). The Lord told the people that He was coming to live among them, making Jerusalem and Judah his "portion in the holy land" (verse 12 NIV).

That's a beautiful promise to an ancient people, but there's also good news for Gentiles today. A time would come when many other people would be joined to the Lord and become His own. Though the ultimate fulfillment of the prophecy remains to be seen, we know that "if anyone acknowledges that Jesus is the Son of God, God lives in them and they in God" (1 John 4:15 NIV).

Today, enjoy all the power and privilege that being one of God's people implies.

WHY DO BAD THINGS HAPPEN?

As Jesus was walking along, he saw a man who had been blind from birth. "Rabbi," his disciples asked him, "why was this man born blind? Was it because of his own sins or his parents' sins?" "It was not because of his sins or his parents' sins," Jesus answered. "This happened so the power of God could be seen in him."

JOHN 9:1–3 NLT

At the Feast of the Tabernacles in Jerusalem, when Jesus encountered a man born blind, the disciples assumed the man's condition was due to sin. But was it the man's own sin or the sin of his parents?

Before we look at Jesus' answer, let's add context to the miracle that followed.

The Feast of the Tabernacles commemorated the Israelites' wilderness experience with people building *sukkot*—frail huts—as they would have had in the wilderness. The feast also featured the drawing of water from the Pool of Siloam and the lighting of lamps at the temple.

After declaring Himself the living water (John 7:37–38) and the light of the world (John 8:12), Jesus was about to heal a man born in darkness with water from Siloam.

Why was this man born blind? So God's power could be shown, testifying the truth about Jesus. He is the living water and the light of the world—a Savior who loves and heals the weak.

When we ask why bad things happen, our focus is in the wrong place. We should ask what God is seeking to do in our troubles. Let's simply believe in His power and rely on His strength to bring us into light and life everlasting.

THEY NEED NOT FEAR

For the LORD God is a sun and shield. The LORD will give grace and glory; no good thing will He withhold from those who walk uprightly. O LORD of hosts, blessed is the man who trusts in You.

PSALM 84:11–12 SKJV

Have you fears about the future? I need not stay to tell you how sweetly the text will lull them all to sleep. Yet suffer me these few sentences.

Do you fear the darkness of future trial? The Lord God is your sun. Do you fear dangers which lie before you in some new sphere upon which you are just entering? The Lord will be your shield. Are there difficulties in your way? Will you need great wisdom and strength? God's grace will be sufficient for you, and His strength will be glorified in your weakness. Do you fear failure? Do you dread final apostasy? It shall not be. He who gives you grace will, without fail, give you glory.

Between here and heaven there is provender for all the flock of God, so that they need not fear famishing on the road. He that leads them shall guide them into pastures that never wither and to fountains that are never dried up, for "no good thing will he withhold from them that walk uprightly."

YES, YOU CAN

Be on guard. Stand firm in the faith.
Be courageous. Be strong.
1 Corinthians 16:13 NLT

Don't believe anyone who tells you the Christian life is easy. In the same way, don't believe anyone who says the Christian life is impossible.

Throughout scripture, we see that God empowers us for His purposes. But He also expects us to do our part. As the apostle Paul said in 1 Corinthians 15:10, "I have worked harder than any of the other apostles; yet it was not I but God who was working through me by his grace" (NLT). Paul did his human part, and God did His divine part. Paul stepped out in faith, and God gave the grace to accomplish tremendous things.

That's why, in today's Bible reading, Paul could issue a string of commands to the Christians of Corinth—and, by extension, to all of us who follow Jesus nearly two thousand years later. "Be on guard. Stand firm in the faith. Be courageous. Be strong." Are those things easy? No. Are they impossible? Absolutely not. Our job is to obey. God's promise is to empower. He will empower as we obey.

Paul's teaching is simply an elaboration of something Jesus Himself said: "All who love me will do what I say. My Father will love them, and we will come and make our home with each of them" (John 14:23 NLT).

If the Trinity is making its home with you, you'll have courage and strength for every trial.

SCRIPTURE INDEX

CONTRIBUTORS

In addition to classic entries from Andrew Murray, Charles Spurgeon, D. L. Moody, and John Wesley, *180 Devotions on Courage for Men* includes the writing of

Bob Evenhouse

David Sanford

Josh Mosey

Lee Warren

Paul Kent

Phil Smouse

Russ Wight

Zech Haynes

MORE ENCOURAGEMENT FOR MEN

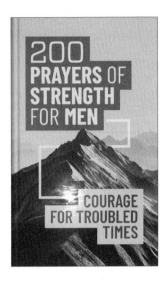

These inspiring prayers and scriptures will turn your eyes from the troubles of this world to the far greater power and glory of your great God. Based on passages from the fresh yet familiar Barbour Simplified King James Version, these prayers offer a powerful jolt of spiritual truth for daily challenges.

Hardback / ISBN 978-1-63609-751-0